PRESENT NAKED!

HOW TO DELIVER YOUR PRESENTATION
WITH SUBSTANCE, STYLE AND SIZZLE!

> Presentation is the "killer skill" we take into the real world.
> It's almost an unfair advantage.
> — *M. Rasiel and Paul N. Friga, Ph.D., The McKinsey World*

BRAD WALDRON

ISBN: 1503303748
ISBN-13: 9781503303744
Library of Congress Control Number: 2014921866
CreateSpace Independent Publishing Platform
North Charleston, South Carolina

"Come to the edge," he said.

"We can't, we're afraid!" they responded.

"Come to the edge," he said.

"We can't, we will fall!" they responded.

"Come to the edge," he said.

And so they came.

And he pushed them.

And they flew."

— Guillaume Apollinaire

Whether you are someone who is already awesome at presenting and are looking for an edge, or you have already begun your presentation journey and want to grow and develop faster, or if you are that person who can think of no terror worse than speaking in front of others, this is for you.

I bow to you. Rei.

ACKNOWLEDGEMENTS

I've had so many great teachers over the years – the best ones have lead through example. There are some people I have worked with that I want to mention because they have inspired and ignited me.

- Howard Eaton and Bob Nishi – My pathfinders in this project.
- Dan Millman – Author, thinker and "Teacher of Occasional Clarity".
- Tony Robbins – A living example of what being the best looks and sounds like.
- Chip Eichelberger – Who inducted me as a foot soldier into Tony's world. You walk your talk.
- Dr Willie Monteiro – No one practices NLP better.
- My Dad – who 'pushed me off the edge' so I could find my voice.

TABLE OF CONTENTS

DO YOU LIGHT UP THE ROOM?

The best way to sell yourself to others
is first to sell the others to yourself.
—NAPOLEON HILL

Some presenters light up the room when they speak, while others only light up the room when they finish. *Present Naked* is about how you can light up a room when you present.

If you're someone who lights up the stage (or podium or meeting room or interview room), you're already familiar with audience applause and return invitations. You've likely been able to do this because you effectively use slides and a script (unwritten or written) to highlight your key points. You've learned not to diminish yourself, and your presentation moves forward. Your audience gets it and you.

But if you're someone who has difficulty lighting up the room, you are probably struggling to engage your audience because you're missing your key points and misusing slides and other media. The harsh reality is that audiences quickly decide whether or not to engage. You can waste lots of time and money preparing an ineffective presentation, and it's no fun feeling you've just been kicked in the seat of your pants.

Present Naked remedies these unnecessary difficulties. My goal is to help you bring out the real you, help you start with a boom, develop your key points, craft scripts and content that get your points across, and end with a bang. As an added bonus, this small book is chock-full of resources, websites, bibliographies, references to other people's books, ideas, talks, and various presentation aids.

Present Naked is for executives, top managers, sales and marketing people, people seeking venture capital, and experts involved in a wide range of presenting. When people have poor presentation skills, time and expenses are wasted, valuable deals are lost, and reputations suffer. This book is aimed at those who

- need to raise their profile;
- have trouble lighting up the room;
- are creating their next talk, presentation, or interview;
- want a simplified approach with a big result; and
- need to overcome their presentation fear.

With products and services becoming more alike and skill sets in the marketplace becoming more comparable, it is crucial that you present yourself well so that you are the one who is hired or the one whose services or products are purchased. The person who *shines* will consistently win.

Present Naked is based on a proven seminar I presented to people wanting to improve their personal presenting skills. You will meet Dante (not his real name) and others who think and comment on what I am saying. Their words and thoughts have been put in italics. *Present Naked* is primarily a conversation between me and people in that class and the personal discoveries they make and implement on their journey.

I have created a website specifically for this book, and each chapter has specific templates, tools, and resources ready to be downloaded as often as you need them. You'll find everything at www.PresentNaked.com. If you're prompted for a password, just type in "brad."

Great speakers. Great talks. Great presentations. Winning interviews. Great sales pitches. Impressed buyers. Engaged audiences. Lighting up the room happens when you know and use the levers of great presenting. You can empower your audiences. You can improve your presence. Enjoy.

Brad Waldron
Angmering, West Sussex, England

CHAPTER 1

THRIVE, SURVIVE, AND NOSE-DIVE

BOOM!

Over thirty million presentations are given every workday around the globe, mostly using PowerPoint software and other graphic media. Sadly, most presentations—in my experience about two-thirds—are mediocre or fail altogether. That's a terrible waste of time, money, and reputation.

Far too many presenters let their presentations become a slide show. And they quickly lose their audiences' engagement and support. Here is what three experts have to say:

- "PowerPoint could be the most powerful tool on your computer. But it's not," says Seth Godin, a marketing expert and successful author. "Countless innovations fail because their champions use PowerPoint the way Microsoft wants them to, instead of the right way."
- "PowerPoint presentations too often resemble a school play," says Edward Tufte, professor emeritus at Yale, "very loud, very slow, and very simple."
- "PowerPoint doesn't kill meetings," says Peter Norvig, Google director of research. "People kill meetings. But using PowerPoint is like having a loaded AK-47 on the table: You can do very bad things with it."

I'm not picking on PowerPoint. It's powerful and useful software for presenting. So, too, is Apple's Keynote, and Prezi (www.Prezi.com) is also starting to make an impact. But as I recently heard Garr Reynolds say at a Presentation Zen talk at an Apple store, "Prezi is starting to cause death by vertigo in presentations!" Too many presentations either nose-dive or are not memorable because presenters kill their presenting. Let's move our expectations up and look at what makes successful presenters.

Have you noticed that some presenters light up the room when they present? And then there are those who only light up the room when they leave.

Those were the first words out of Brad's mouth, and I found myself chuckling a little, knowing very well what he was talking about. The rest of the class laughed, too. We had all seen presenters so terrible that we were relieved when they finally walked off the stage.

The good news is that excellent, mediocre, or bad presenting is a choice. You simply choose to be the best possible you. If you can do that, you will shine.

The first decision you must make even before you stand up and present is to simply accept that you have all the resources you need to deliver an outstanding presentation. The question we must ask ourselves is: Are we tapping into our best resources to gain that advantage when we present? If we are not, then we are not being truthful to ourselves.

I thought of myself as a decent presenter, but I knew that I wasn't performing to my full potential, which was why I had decided to attend Brad's course.

THRIVE, SURVIVE, OR NOSE-DIVE

Some presenters thrive, they get into a perfect flow and their audiences love it; others nose-dive and unhappily lose their audiences—and their confidence; some presenters just survive, though the reasons for such mediocrity often go unidentified. I'll spend more time on Survive than Thrive and Nose-Dive, but first I want to share a story about Kate.

KATE

There were two candidates left for the job as a key director in a global organization. The hot favorite, Kate, had the experience, exposure, skills, and energy to take this job. On paper and in interviews, she demonstrated the job was hers to lose. The other candidate also had solid credentials but not as robust as Kate's. The final interview requirement involved presenting to a panel of decision makers.

The presentations were done immediately after each other to ensure complete objectivity from the panel. Kate presented second. But the unthinkable happened. Kate left her presenting skills in the parking lot. It would be fair to say that she was decidedly mediocre. Kate's competence was in setting a compelling vision and achieving objectives, not in winning an intellectual beauty parade. At least that was what Kate said the recruiter told her when he informed her that she hadn't gotten the job.

"Are you sure it was your presenting?" I asked Kate.

"The HR director told me," Kate said. "The other candidate won the job by presenting well when it mattered most. He lit up the presentation room and I didn't—it was clear to everyone."

All was not lost. The HR director saw plenty of potential in Kate and offered her a different job. She accepted the job of category controller, not category director, the job she really wanted.

The school of hard knocks is a school from which we never graduate. There is always another skill we can learn. As Kate's new life began, one of her goals was to become a champion presenter. That was about six years ago.

Kate's story struck home because something similar had happened to me. I had lost a job opportunity, a job I really wanted. Though I thought of myself as a decent presenter, I knew I wasn't presenting to my full potential. Again, that's why I decided to attend Brad's course. Still skeptical, I continued listening, but he was interesting and he still had my attention.

3

Most presenters fit into the category called Survive—for very important reasons, but first I want to deal with Thrive and Nose-Dive. Imagine a bell curve and let Thrive and Nose-Dive form its opposite ends.

Bell Curve

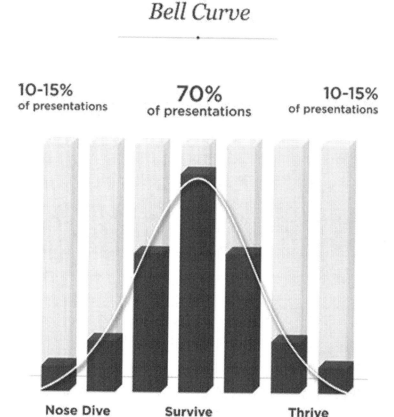

| **10-15%** | **70%** | **10-15%** |
| of presentations | of presentations | of presentations |

Nose Dive   Survive   Thrive

THRIVE

Thrive is a wondrous category—presenters pray for this one. You know when your content and your style are thriving because it's energizing you and your audience; people are captivated by your presentation. It's as though time stops. It's not any one thing that may be special; it's just that everything is flowing. People find you personable and impactful, the content is spot on, and the medium illustrates your key points perfectly. That's a thriving presentation. Here's a question. Out of the last ten presentations you've seen, how many would you rate in the Thrive category?

I had seen some great presentations that were genuinely engaging and worthwhile, but I could only recall a few. The rest of the class had experienced the same thing. Not many, I said. Others in the class concurred.

NOSE-DIVE

At the other end of the spectrum, there's Nose-Dive. And most audiences vividly remember these presentations for all the wrong reasons! You know when a Nose Dive is happening. They stand out and are painful to watch.

Here's an example of a Nose Dive, one I witnessed. A young guy came along for a job interview with me for a training facilitator's role. I've always felt that one of the best ways to interview a presenter is to ask him or her to facilitate a session. It's like an audition. Here's how Trevor (not his real name) started his session.

"Hi, my name is Trevor, umm. I've always believed that it's good to start a presentation with a joke. Umm, here's a joke for you," he said, reading from a scrap of paper. "How much is a bird in the hand worth?" His audience remained silent. "Nothing because it's dead," Trevor said lamely. "It's not worth anything—it's dead. So, welcome!"

Sadly, that was verbatim how he opened his presentation. That's not what I'd call even a Survive presentation—never mind Thrive. Trevor didn't get much further in that facilitation. Though well intended, his opening was awful, totally unprofessional. With coaching, he improved, but on this particular day he certainly did a Nose Dive.

Just as I had seen great presentations, I had also seen truly terrible ones, the kind that make you want to sneak out the back door to escape. I looked around and saw the other people in my class silently nodding in agreement. We all knew about Nose Dives. They occur when your opening is lousy, you miss your key points, your slides or graphics confuse the audience, and you haven't thought out your script—what you're going to say.

I wondered what he had to say about the Survive category.

SURVIVE

I left this category for last, because it describes that vast middle part of the bell curve. It's what I affectionately call no-man's-land. This is where you've completed an acceptable presentation, you've left, and people feel that it was nice. Then a week later, some people will struggle to remember what your presentation was about! The moment you get that response, you know your presentation was a Survive experience.

Most presentations aren't memorable—not great, not terrible, merely adequate. I'll admit that I've given mediocre presentations too. We've all had plenty of room to improve. There are many examples of Survive. Here are some causes of Survive presenting:

- using humor at the expense of presenting real content
- using too many slides and graphics
- using mediocre openings and closing
- failing to earn and maintain your audience's interest
- presenting in a flat and monotone way

There was a rumble of general agreement from the class. We'd all witnessed those causes. Brad clapped his hands.

Let's do an exercise. I've got a chart here—it's on the opposite page, with rows for Thrive, Survive, and Nose-Dive and columns for style, content, and audiovisuals. I want you to write down responses, behaviors, and feelings you've gotten from past presenters you've experienced. Put them on the chart.

EXERCISE: Thrive, Survive, and Nose-Dive

	STYLE	CONTENT	AUDIOVISUAL
THRIVE	1	2	3
SURVIVE	4	5	6
NOSE-DIVE	7	8	9

(Note: Readers, you can do this exercise. Go to www.bradwaldron.co.uk/index.php/materials and click on the slide deck, "Thriving Presentations." You will be able to download the worksheets for this exercise.)

BOX 1

If you saw a Thrive presentation, what *behaviors* were exhibited when the presenter opened his or her talk, presentation, or interview? Write as many as you can think of. As a target, aim for ten.

It could be as follows:

➤ Passion

➤ Great eye contact

➤ Natural body language

BOX 2

If you saw a presentation where the person's *content* thrived, what sort of content was presented? Write as many as you can think of. As a target, aim for ten.

➤ Up-to-date

➤ Personally relevant

➤ Insightful

BOX 3

If you saw a presentation where the person's audiovisual (AV) usage thrived, how did that person handle the slides? What made the slides so effective? Write as many as you can think of. Rate the categories one through ten.

➤ Beautiful slides

➤ The story flowed via the slides

➤ Right microphone volume

Do the same for the Survive and Nose-Dive sections.

You may discover a huge range of differences in each box, and I would expect that to be the case. However, everything you write in the Thrive boxes won't suit everyone. For instance, being humorous can be a great part of a thriving style. However, for an inexperienced presenter, using humor could be the thing that creates a Nose-Dive experience for them.

Once you have filled in the table, put your reflective hat on and ask yourself (or ask people who have experienced you presenting) to tick the individual things they see you do in any of the boxes. By doing that, you'll gain a pretty good understanding of how you mostly present. If experience is anything to go by, I would imagine you'll find ticks everywhere. But here is the *secret* to this exercise. If you have ticks in the Survive and Nose-Dive boxes, don't worry. Forget about it. Yes, really forget about it. *Pay more attention to where there are* no *ticks in the Thrive row.* That's because your pot of gold resides there—in the Thrive category. If you focused your development on the elements within the Thrive category, you'll be halfway there to delivering world-class presentations. And it's my bet that all the ingredients in the Thrive section are totally within your capabilities. It just takes a bit of coaching and practice.

Look at your chart. Do you notice something? Here's the chart with all of your work on it.

Some ingredients to help you thrive...

	Style	Content	Medium
Thrive	Natural with right energy Charismatic Happy and Personable Resonate vocal qualities Impactful and Confident Passionate Rapport with audience	Relevant Chunked correctly Sign posted Clear outcomes Understandable Engaging Natural conclusion	Clean slides Good acoustics Appropriate lighting Clear line of view of speaker Right temperature Comfortable seating High quality AV
Survive	Flat energy Monotone Lack of audience connection Talks to the screen Shuffles No eye contact Moves around aimlessly	No clear objectives Lots of content and data Too little data Content is like a monologue Lacks direction Not relevant to group Doesn't meet groups needs	Slides are "6 points with 6 words" Occasional speaker sound feedback Projection not fitting the screen size The AV is the presentation not the speaker
Nose Dive	Noticably nervous Arrogant Rude and confrontationable Distracting habits Not prepared Patronising Trying to be someone else	Endless drivel Out of date Wrong Boring Transparent No value Irrelevant	Uncomfortable temperature Death by PowerPoint Sound system ineffective Equipment not working Room too dark Over complicated Room too crowded

We looked over our chart, and some people raised their hands. "I see lots of sticky notes in the Thrive row," Amanda said. "There are also a lot of sticky notes in the Nose-Dive row," I said.

Brad asked us what else we noticed. "What are those cartoon characters in the Survive row?" I asked. Brad had done something that surprised all of us; he had placed twelve cartoon characters across the Survive row over the work we had already done.

Thrive and Nose-Dive are straightforward; they're either great, or they suck. The tricky thing is really identifying what makes a presentation fall into the Survive category. It's almost worse than a Nose Dive, in a way. It's like a lingering death. It's where most presenters go and die—an avoidable boneyard. There is something about presentations where the presenter is just surviving. It's difficult to identify what went wrong, but you know it wasn't successful.

This brings me to archetype presenters. *Avoid these twelve archetypes.*

THE TWELVE ARCHETYPES

Take a careful look at each archetype. We've all been there at one time or another: a darkened conference room, a slightly glazed look in your eyes, looking at and listening to a person present, but not really hearing what he or she is saying. Instead, we're distracted by the presenter's method of presenting—his or her body movements or tone of voice. Often, how people present is a product of nervousness and an uneducated presentation style. Over the last fifteen years I've noticed that these twelve archetypes fill presenting stages every day. Some of us have a repertoire combining several archetypes, and they limit our presenting effectiveness, condemning us to Survival.

Consider the twelve presenting styles listed below and see if you recognize whether you fit into one or more of them.

THE CHILDREN'S PRESENTER

The Children's Presenter is generally someone looking for affirmation. She bounces around and says things like, "Right, hello everyone. Hey, how's everyone this morning? Are we feeling good?" It's a type of style you see on Sesame Street, Play School, or CBBC. Whatever credibility the audience gives to this kind of presenter is soon lost.

THE PRESENTATION THIEF

This archetype is a lot more discreet. The Presentation Thief sneaks up on you. You sit there and you're actually enjoying yourself and you think the presentation is good, but then you realize that while you've been entertained, the presentation lacked value and substance. The presenter has stolen valuable time from your life, and you suddenly realize it—usually after he has left. This archetype is usually a good entertainer—often a jokester—and uses entertainment to win the audience. But key points are glossed over or missed altogether.

THE DANCER

The Dancer is one of the most common types of presenter. This presenter can't stand still; she needs to move, and her movements aren't random. The person presenting is literally dancing on stage, doing the 1960s dance called the Shadow Step: step forward on your right foot, swing your left over your right, step back with the right, step back with the left, and then start again. Most audiences find a dancing presenter distracting and ultimately an amateur.

THE PUPPY DOG

This archetype gets up and looks at the audience with big doe eyes, and the audience instinctively knows the presenter is nervous and vulnerable. The Puppy Dog tries to sell you on his emotional weakness and often starts the presentation with "This is my first presentation," or "I'm not a professional speaker." Have you seen this archetype? This type is grounded in pure fear,

THE NEWS READER

The News Reader really perplexes me. A good deal of competence is normally associated with the News Reader, and quite often presenters like this have attended a presentation skills course or two that endorses such a delivery. Their presenting is starchy in style and robotic. My concern is that while

News Readers project a professional image, they mask their real personality, which is a problem of many authoritative figures, such as leaders, top managers, and experts.

THE TOP GUN PILOT

Then we have the Top Gun Pilot, a common form of presenting. I have some good friends who use the Top Gun style. These types of presenters are most famous for their lack of preparation; they thrive on adrenaline and end up "winging" the presentation. Executives, top managers, and experts frequently resort to this archetypal style of presentation. One problem is that their presentations are all about them, their accomplishments and top gun knowledge.

THE MOTOR MOUTH

The Motor Mouth is an annoying form of presenting. This presenter gets up, presents, and hardly stops for a breath. Even though you may want to ask a question, you feel it's rude because the presenter is on such a roll. And she thinks she's on a roll. But what the Motor Mouth is doing is going a million miles an hour ahead of her audience, leaving them behind—struggling, confused, and disengaged.

THE DRAMATIST

The Dramatist is full of flair and delivers a presentation in an over-the-top way. Like a frustrated actor, this type of presenter tries to please and deliver with impact, but alas, his best efforts get mocked.

THE CAGED TIGER

Closely related to the Dancer, the Caged Tiger paces from side to side across her speaking space—usually looking at the floor while speaking. It's distracting for the audience. This presenting archetype is usually covering up nervousness and insufficient rehearsal.

THE LION KING

Then there's the Lion King, an alpha personality, the big lion, roaring, "Right, here's what we're going to do today. Got it?" His presence demands authority and *control*. The king barks orders and expects immediate obedience.

Do you remember the movie *The Bridge over the River Kwai*? Alec Guinness loses sight of his mission and misleads his soldiers. This frequently happens with this kind of presenter. The messenger becomes the message, misses key points, and loses the support of the audience.

THE NERVOUS NELLY

This problem is shared by most beginning presenters. They stutter, their palms glisten with sweat, they may have a flushed face, and their voice quivers. The audience quickly picks up on their nervous disposition. When I first started training and presenting twenty years ago, there were times when I'd walk on stage and literally be wringing wet, absolutely drenched.

THE SLIDE JUNKIE

Last but not least, there's the Slide Junkie. This presenter spends more time facing the screen than facing her audience. These presenters love their slides; they hide behind them and find safety in doing so.

Since the advent of PowerPoint and similar software, more good presentations are wrecked by a host of special features: spinning objects and words, inappropriate music, flashing slides, and unnecessary video inserts. To make matters worse, too many Slide Junkie presenters lose control of their remotes or AV protocols.

In the real world real, people struggle to present well, and so they resort to these archetypes, which diminish the impact of their presentation and increase their presenting problems. It's a critical issue because the inability to present well also diminishes the reputation of the organization the presenter represents. Presenting is worth mastering.

In my classes I ask my students which archetypes they identify with. Speaking for myself, there is an element of the Dramatist in me, and I have to be careful with that.

The class started confessing.

"At times I've deliberately been the Puppy Dog," someone said. *"The first time I delivered to our French team, I came across as the stupid English person bumbling through. I stood there with this doe-eyed, dim-witted look on my face that came across as, "I'm really sorry, I'm English."*

"I'm a Dancer," another person said. "I can't keep my feet in one position for very long, and it's not that I'm moving in a particular shape; I will move everywhere. I know it drives people crazy. It's something I want to work on."

"I'm used to winging it with a combination of the Motor Mouth and Caged Tiger pacing back and forth," another person said.

One attendee owned up to being a total Slide Junkie and laughed, wincing at how he must have looked to his audience.

TWO ASPECTS OF A SURVIVAL PRESENTATION

Although avoiding each of the twelve archetypes can help prevent a Nose Dive, I believe presenters use the archetypes as a Survival strategy and for two main reasons:

- They are easily learned behaviors.
- They are coping strategies.

The most important aspect is that archetypes are really coping strategies. I dare say with most of them we could analyze them and identify what drives someone to use one or more of the archetypes. Over time as we face one or more of our presenting monsters, we compensate and resort to them. They help us cope—but not win. Archetypes are the enemies of being able to Present Naked.

For instance, the Puppy Dog presenter has learned to get acceptance by asking the audience to "cuddle and pet me." The Children's Entertainer likes to see people smile, so she gets right up there and says, "Hi, ladies and gentle-men, welcome," and whoever in the audience smiles the most winsomely at her becomes her connection. Sometimes people combine one or more of these archetypes.

This brings me back to an important presenting principle: *Be yourself.*

It was at this point I realized that Brad was encouraging us—me—not to hide behind an archetype, but to let our true selves out for our audiences to see, hear, and connect with.

I raised my hand. "How do we break a bad presenting habit?" I asked.

There was general interest in my question.

Remember Kate? The first thing we did together was break Kate's arche-type patterns. They were so ingrained she couldn't see them. In the English countryside the farmers have a wonderful though earthy expression, "A fox can't smell its own muck [poo!]." That translates into we can't see our own blind spots.

THE LAW OF OVERCOMPENSATION

I use a coaching principle to smash dysfunctional archetypes. The princi-ple is called the law of overcompensation. For example, assume you're a tennis player and you unintentionally keep serving the ball to the left of your target. I could just try to help you modify your technique, but in my experience, that never rarely works in correcting a habit of bad serving.

Instead, I do the total opposite. I get the person to deliberately serve to the extreme right of the target. They do that until they become an expert at serving the ball in the opposite direction. At that point I casually say, "Do me a favor, serve the ball into the original target space." Guess what happens? A near perfect serve occurs.

The same principle applies with eliminating an archetype. When I am coaching someone and witness an archetype dominating his presentation style, I ask him to do the opposite of the archetype. For example, I ask the

Children's Presenter to pretend she is the Lion King. Doing this helps people to push through their own bad habits and perceived limits and helps restore a balanced approach to their natural style.

UNLOCKING A DYSFUNCTIONAL ARCHETYPE

Let's do a personal exercise that will help achieve two outcomes:

1.Understand what *causes* you to drop into an archetype.
2. Identify what resources you need to develop better behaviors.

The good news about this exercise is you can do it in the privacy of your own mind. I am going to take you on a short visualization. You will go on a mental excursion: you are going to have a look at what it's like when you are presenting in the style of one of the archetypes.

First, sit in a way that makes you feel comfortable and close your eyes. Take a nice deep breath, and as you exhale, allow yourself to relax even more. Imagine you're sitting in a wonderful cinema. You're sitting in a place where you have a full view of the screen. The images on the screen are in black and white, and the sound is not too loud, just nice and pleasant sounding.

As you sit looking at the screen, project onto it a time when you did a presentation and an archetype was present during the presentation. You might discover that quite a few archetypes were displaying themselves in this presentation, and that's OK.

Notice how you move in that archetype, how you feel when you're that archetype. When you notice those things, push the pause button on your presentation and ask yourself, "What is the trigger that causes this archetype or collection of archetypes to come into me?"

There was a long pause after Brad asked us to do this, and I could hear people's chairs shifting around the room. I wanted to open my eyes to see what was going on, but I had enough trust in what Brad was doing to stay for the full journey with my eyes closed. As I was looking at my archetype I noticed that I started to do the Dancer at the point when I was feeling anxious about my next slide. What a revelation! The archetype came out when I was feeling most vulnerable. I thought the archetype was just a style that I had developed. But now, as I watched myself present, it became really obvious that the archetype was a coping strategy, a way to help me to deal with my nerves. Brad started speaking again.

As you sit comfortably in your chair thinking about your archetype, think about what triggers that archetype and why it appears. For some of us, it's a collection of habits that have appeared over time; for others, it could be a simple coping strategy to help deal with nerves, and perhaps for some of us it may be a sign that we've got too much energy, which has led to anxiety. The archetype becomes a way to dissipate that energy.

Now make the film go backward just to that time before the archetype made its appearance, and then hit pause once you get to that place. In the comfort of your chair, ask yourself this question: What resources does the you on the screen need to be confident, to be present in the moment, and to be perfectly natural when you present? Think about that now. Maybe there is a list of things or maybe just one thing that will make all the difference. Just know that deep inside you have all the resources you need to be a confident and effective presenter. Consider the skills, attitudes, and temperaments you need to be the best presenter you can be. It is these attributes that will override the archetypes and help you raise your skills up to the Thrive level. Place these attributes into yourself in the movie you are watching and notice the difference it will make in how you deliver your presentation.

Press the play button again and watch your presentation with you presenting once more, but this time free of the archetypes and full of the very things that show you to be confident, articulate, engaging, and effective. Watch the whole film through now and notice how you move with these new skills, how you speak with these new skills. Notice how people respond to you with this better style of presenting. How good does that feel? Also notice how easy you make great presentations look. Well done. And when you feel that achieving this way of presenting is within you, slowly open your eyes and have a gentle stretch.

That was deep. There I was one minute nervously dancing around, and the next minute I was entertaining and engaging. I actually feel right now as if I could get up and present passionately and with confidence. I looked around the room and I noticed everyone had a glow about them. Sure, there were a few nervous-looking smiles, but by and large, everyone looked confident and had big smiles on their faces.

"Well done, everybody! Thank you for trusting me enough to go on that little journey. While I was watching everyone during that process, it was clear to me some of you went on quite a deep journey. Some of you may have felt a bit uncomfortable. Whatever happened to you was right for you," said Brad. "Let's talk about what happened during the experience. Who made some discoveries about the archetypes that were inside them and more importantly what triggers the archetype?"

One lady said, "I got embarrassed watching myself present, and then when I saw that I was a Slide Junkie, it made me cringe. But then I realized the reason I did that was because if I looked at people and if they did look interested, I think I would collapse in a bundle of nerves."

"That's a great realization," Brad said. "May I ask, what did you do in the second part of that process when you had the resources you needed to overcome the archetype?"

"At first my mind went blank. I didn't know what resources could help me. And then as I relaxed a little bit more, I noticed that if I had the confidence I had when I played netball and was shooting for a goal that would help me look out to the audience and not look at the screen. So when I imagined that confidence and put it into my presentation and then played the movie again, I didn't even look at the screen once. In fact, I was confident, flowing, and I was actually enjoying my presentation, and even better than that, so was the audience!"

The group laughed out loud. "Hands up who had a similar experience?" asked Brad. Everyone put their hands up, including me!

I have some good news to you, this is the start of our journey together, and from here we're going to look at the most effective, powerful, and engaging resource you have at your disposal it's called—be *you!*

FREQUENTLY ASKED QUESTIONS

Q. **What do you mean when you say that it's my choice?**

A. It's your choice whether you want to create a memorable impression with your audience. If you want to be memorable, then don't, for example, rely on slides: slides are only a part of how you get messages across. Other things are involved, especially connecting with your audience and engaging with them. It's your choice.

Q. **Thrive is where I'd like to be. Should I get a professional to help me?**

A. Good coaching always adds value, but you can't delegate the tasks of developing an outstanding presentation. Do the hard work yourself. *You are the presenter.*

Q. **How do I know that my past presentations thrived?**

A. Think of your last few presentations and rate their style, content, and the audiovisuals and what you remember of your audiences' responses and evaluations (if you have the latter). When you assess your presentations, be rigorous and search for a true analysis.

Q. **What should I concentrate my efforts on regarding improvement?**

A. Take the exercise outlined in this chapter called Thrive, Survive, and Nose-Dive. You'll see a number of blanks in the Thrive boxes. Pay more attention to where the ticks are *not* in your Thrive boxes because that's where your pot of gold resides—in the Thrive section. Those qualities are what you will want to spend most of your time and efforts developing

Q. **I was interested in the archetypes. I see several that describe me. Is the point to avoid any of those characteristics? Can they be avoided?**

A. Yes. I hope that's one of the reasons you're reading this book. The point is to become unlike any of the archetypes. And you can undo such problems. Do it well, and your presentations stand a good chance of thriving, which is the point. You can avoid the boredom of just surviving and the disasters of nose-diving. You can do it.

Q. **I've seen other personal coaches use your law of overcompensation. Is your approach something like NLP?**

A. Yes. If that's the way you want to think about it, fine. It works. But in matters of presenting, if you want to get rid of Survive or Nose-Dive archetypal behaviors, identify your archetype and change your behavior. It's important to practice a correcting behavior until it becomes natural to you. Sometimes when we try to change something about ourselves, what is actually right may feel wrong. And what is wrong (the old limiting behavior) actually feels right.

CHAPTER 2

JUST YOU

Do your own thinking. Be the chess player,
not the chess piece.

—RALPH CHARELL

BANG!

Great presenters are born, but just as importantly, they are *made* as well. The most important skill is learning to be just you.

When you Present Naked, you are accomplishing exactly that—being the best person you can possibly be, yourself. Free from anything you are not, just being you. And that's key: being more of you is liberating. Once you let go of the (ego-driven) need of having to be the best presenter or slavishly copying someone else, a freedom and truth is released into your presentation, and your audience responds favorably. That's what Present Naked is all about—being totally natural, just being you.

Present Naked is in essence being who you really are when you present. But first you must rid yourself of three presentation myths and remember three truths.

MYTH

"Only experienced, confident people give good presentations."

TRUTH

Everyone has feelings of self-doubt at some point. Learn to use fear as an enabler and turn it into confidence.

MYTH

"My presenting style is not as good as others."

TRUTH

Being *you* is the best person you'll ever need to be! In my experience, most people don't let their real selves shine through, but you can change that.

MYTH

"People will think I'm boring."

TRUTH

You choose your presentation style without regard for the content. Being boring is a skill, and some people actually practice it; sometimes not on purpose, but that's what they do!

In this book we will explore gaining presentation confidence, principles that increase your personal power, where confidence comes from, and how to get it. We'll also look at your beliefs about yourself as a presenter and whether they help or hinder. The objective is to examine how to bring more of the *real you* into the presentation.

THREE PRINCIPLES THAT INCREASE YOUR PERSONAL POWER

Here are important fundamentals of Present Naked:

1. Be more of you.
2. Be confident.
3. Be present—something that escapes too many presenters.

When you incorporate these three principles into your presentations, you can increase your power, effectiveness, and personal enjoyment. Let's explore them further.

1. BE MORE OF YOU

Being yourself is all you will ever need. However, most people need to let out more of who they really are. The more your personality connects with the audience, the more they will bond with you and feel comfortable with you. It will build your likeability.

As he said those words, I realized that he did act completely natural and that I felt comfortable listening to him as well. I wanted to develop that kind of powerful connection with my audience. Before I could ponder the point further, Brad went on to the next principle.

2. BE CONFIDENT

Learn to be comfortable in front of an audience. It takes practice and experience. If you feel tentative, don't worry. You can gain confidence, but be careful not to go too far—to the point of arrogance or cockiness. Audiences hate arrogance, but they love confidence when it is genuine.

I wanted to be more confident, and I was eager to learn more about it. Brad made it look easy; whatever technique he was using seemed to be working.

3. BE PRESENT

Presenting in the moment is the source of a great presenter's strength. He's free from fear, distraction, worry, and anything else that can take him out of his zone. This is a critical point. The Japanese have the perfect word for being present—*nagare,* which means "flow."

I first came across *nagare* from a sports perspective, specifically from martial arts. Dan Millman, an early mentor of mine, taught a knife-fighting seminar called "Courage Training." At the end of a week's training, you had to fight three attackers. Each had a knife. If you were anywhere other than in the moment, you fell on a knife—a limp rubber one though! It was through Dan I learned the value of *nagare* and how it relates to presenting. When you think about it, most problems occur during a presentation because people aren't in the moment.

Here's a question for everyone: Who's ever had something go wrong during a presentation? I know I have. Think about it: What went wrong? Were you worrying about something while you were presenting? Did you get distracted by something outside yourself?

There's a saying in the acting world: "Never work with animals or children." In the presenting world, I sometimes feel there should be a similar principle, something like: "Never work with someone else's computer and sound system."

Recently I worked with Dame Ellen Macarthur and her charity for children with cancer (www.ellenmacarthurtrust.org). She was traveling around the coast of Britain with a bunch of kids on a yacht to help raise money and awareness. Whenever we pulled into a port, Ellen did a presentation to the general public and yachting enthusiasts. One day we docked at Dover on the south coast of England and presented to a full house. My role that day was to warm up the audience and create some expectations by showing a video clip of Ellen out on the seas winning various global races—and then introduce Ellen. On this occasion I announced the video clip, and it came on in black and white and with no sound. For those wondering, it was supposed to be in color and have sound.

I was standing to the left of the screen watching this video in black and white with no sound thinking, *oh, my God!* (or words to that effect). Realizing I was on the verge of a massive panic attack, I looked at the audience and thought, the audience doesn't know it was supposed to be in color and with sound. So I then thought, how wonderful! It looks like a real moody introduction! Crisis over, I told myself; just stay present and enjoy the video from a different perspective.

That is, until my dear friend Jo Bootle yelled from the audiovisual technical room at the back of the auditorium, "Brad. We've lost the sound, and it's in black and white!" Any panic would be warranted at this point, I thought. It's one thing if I know there's a problem; it's quite another when the audience knows. *Stay present and breathe*, I told myself.

At that point I decided I had to work with the problem and not ignore it. By now, all two hundred guests were aware there was a problem. In a cheeky tone, I said to Jo via the microphone so everyone could hear, "Actually Jo, I prefer it like this—it adds more drama. And besides, I don't think the audience realizes it's not working properly. So if we pretend it's normal, we may just get away with it!"

The audience erupted with laughter. I then asked for the lights to be put back on, apologized for the technical issue, remarked that I was actually enjoying the film clip in its new medium, and said the technical issue would soon get resolved. I continued on with my next section of the introduction, which involved the work the charity did, and by the time I had concluded, the video was ready to run again, but this time in color and with sound.

Errors will occur. The error is rarely the real problem. How you respond is the real moment of truth. In this situation, I had responded with *negare*. When you are more of yourself—confident and present—you will be a powerful and effective presenter, a *Naked* Presenter.

I was beginning to understand what Brad meant by Present Naked, and I wanted to hear more. If what he was describing were possible, it would definitely be worth my time and effort.

COUNT TO TEN

Moving on, let's discuss the next principle of being more of *you*. For this I'll need everyone on their feet.

We got up, wondering what he had in mind for us. Since this was a course in presenting, I wondering if we were going have to present ourselves.

We're all going to do is something very simple. And it's something that we can all easily achieve. First, let's count from 1 to 10. However, we won't just count from 1 to 10. I want you to start at number 1 with a whisper. By the time you get to 10, be as loud as you can be. So from 1 and 10 gradually get louder. Who will to lead?

Utter silence filled the room. No one volunteered. I finally whispered, one, two, and then everyone joined in. Three. Four. Five. The counting grew faster and faster and our voices rose to a roar.

"Six, seven, eight, nine, ten!" People were out of breath. A few giggled when we were through.

"How did it feel to get to ten?" Brad asked.

"Good," said one man with a grin.

"We built up momentum," a woman observed.

"Exactly," Brad said. "And what would happen if I asked you to do it by yourself in front of all of us?"

The smiles faded.

"Not so good," someone mumbled.

"Why?" Brad challenged. "What's different?"

"You're out on your own," someone said.

Others chimed in: "No support." "People are going to judge you if you don't go loud enough."

"Yeah, what if they don't like your ten?" I said to Brad. My fear is the audience not liking my ten.

"Good point," Brad said. "The fear of you not liking my 9 or 10 means I'm going to pitch an 8. What I find is that people hold back, and they're actually being an 8 when they say they're being a 10."

He was right. I hadn't really shouted as loud as I could; I had held back. I realized that I frequently hold back when I present.

3 ZONES OF COMFORT

First, learn to be yourself—squarely inside the Me zone. That's your comfort zone. The aim then is to expand gradually into the Not Me space but avoid going into the Panic space. Here's a graphic that may help.

Zones of Comfort

THE PANIC SPACE

This is where presenters experience mental and emotional paralysis and pure fear. You can learn to avoid such experiences.

Panic is a self-induced state. It generally occurs when the voices inside your head are much louder than the words coming out of your mouth. Think of the times when you have panicked and ask yourself why you panicked. Who has panicked or has seen a friend panic?

There was a silence in the room that was deafening. Then a timid voice beside me said, "I started stuttering once when my boss asked me some detail behind some financial figures I was presenting, and I didn't have the data to hand."

"That sounds very exposing and potentially very vulnerable. What did you do?" Brad asked with an open concern.

"Well, I started to shuffle through my notes, hoping the figures would magically appear because I didn't know what else to do. To be honest, I almost cried."

"That sounds like a horrible experience. Potentially bad enough to install a phobia about every wanting to present again for fear of being exposed."

"That's exactly right! I don't want to present anymore. I'll do anything to get out of presenting now."

That, my friends, is the main long-term consequence of entering the panic zone during a presentation: it can lead to developing a phobia about public speaking. It's bad enough having the hallucinations about public speaking and presentations but to have a real memory about it all going wrong is potentially a future obstacle.

THE NOT ME SPACE

In this space presenters are uncomfortable, and they feel their presenting is wrong or embarrassing them or exposing them to negative audience reactions.

Stay with the counting 1 to 10 exercise for a moment; learn to expand outside your comfort zone, to really stretch out into the 8, 9, and 10 range. But the 1, 2, and 3 range is important as well. This scale of 1 to 10 applies not only to the volume of your voice but to everything—gestures, intensity, and emotions that you use when you present. When you get into the 8, 9, 10 counting space, I call that the Not Me space. Because it doesn't feel comfortable or safe, we cannot identify with it, so it literally causes our thinking to decide this is Not Me. Don't get me wrong: I don't think anyone ever needs to scream 8, 9, 10 in a presentation, but there are things we all need to do that will feel not safe but are the very thing we need to do to be a more effective presenter. In other words, I want to see more of the real you come through. I want you to expand your range.

Some common situations that cause people to be in the Not Me space are as follows:

- taking questions from the audience
- presenting with spotlights on them
- presenting someone else's presentation

Making larger gestures than normal and adding more vocal variety while presenting can also throw a presenter into a Not Me space.

I was curious to see how Brad would apply this idea of expanding our range to all the aspects of a presentation. That would be dynamic and engaging.

THE ME SPACE

This is where presenters are comfortable and enjoy themselves, like being in the flow, experiencing *nagare*. Our goal is to expand the Me space into the Not Me space—and that requires confidence mixed with a bit of an appetite for risk.

HOW TO BE MORE CONFIDENT

There are courses, therapies, and hundreds of books on the next principle of Present Naked, It's probably the most desired outcome of all presentation programs—it's how to be more confident when you present. I think confidence is so important when it comes to everything in life, and I want to share some life-changing distinctions about what it is, where it comes from, and, more importantly, how you get it.

When I was a teenager, my number-one fear by a country mile was speaking up for myself. The thought of having to call a movie theater to find out what time a film was being shown sent me into total paralysis. The same happened with public speaking; unfortunately, I didn't realize that it sent me into a paralysis until I actually had to stand up and try to speak at a school debate. I was fifteen. I was a mess: my palms were wet with sweat. I was living proof of the power of thoughts. Because public speaking was so debilitating for me, I made it a mission to learn how to overcome this phobia. Now I want to share with everyone a few gold nuggets so that being confident is a natural and seamless choice. First of all, let's look at *how* we produce fears and confidence.

THOUGHTS, BEHAVIOR, AND PHYSIOLOGY

We experience the world through our five senses, and we filter what we see based on our own bias, values, goals, and experience. That's why some people find babies cute, and other people don't see babies as being cute. Nevertheless, how we perceive the world drives the *quality* of our thinking.

Blueprint

Internal Thoughts

Internal State

Behavior

Physiology

Thoughts are real forces

BLUEPRINT OF THOUGHT

Let's do an example together. I'll say a sentence, and let's see what impact it has on everyone. Here's one, "I've booked sky diving for this afternoon!" What are you thinking?

I've got images of me dying was my immediate response. Another response was, I can't wait to tell my partner. It certainly aroused a variety of internal thoughts in everyone.

Now, notice how those thoughts have made you feel. How do you feel about skydiving?

I feel sick, I said. I feel excited, said another person. Other responses varied between these two extremes, but most responses were negative.

31

Do you see? Not only notice how it made you feel, notice how it's affected your physiology. Look at the people who feel sick and scared. What do you notice about them? They're slumped in their chairs. They've gone pale. Their faces are covered in distress. Contrast that to the people who are excited. They're sitting upright in their chairs, have a positive physiological response, and their bodies seem filled with energy.

Here's the killer fact in this model: What *you think* drives how you feel, and how you feel drives the quality of what you do. So what am I really saying? Thoughts are real forces.

This means if you want to give a great presentation, you have to be in a great state. The way to get into a great state is to either manage your physiology and/or manage the quality of your thoughts. It's easy to understand at a conceptual level, but it can be a challenge when you're about to walk on stage or stand before an interview panel.

THE POWER OF THOUGHTS

Let's test the power of this model. I need a demonstration subject who has given a strong presentation where he or she was filled confidence.

I volunteered.

You're the perfect volunteer, Dante, because you're a big strapping man, and I'm going to show how—in just thirty seconds—I can make you as half as strong as you are just by asking you a couple of questions.

Here's what I want you to do: hold one arm out straight to the side and make it as strong as you can. Then I'm going to push that arm down by your side. All you have to do is resist my pushing.

But before he pushed my arm down, Brad first asked me to think about my positive presentation and remember what it was like and how it made me feel. While I thought about my successful presentation, Brad tried to push my arm down, but he had a real struggle because of how strong I was.

Well done. You're amazingly strong but not for much longer. I'm going to do the same exercise with Dante, but this time I'm going to ask him to think of a truly poor presentation he's given.

He pushed down again. My arm collapsed like a youngster's. This can't be true, I thought.

I'd like everyone to pair and have a go at this exercise. However, this time, I don't want you to tell the person pushing down on your arm whether you are thinking of a good or bad presentation. Just think of one of them and have the other person push down on your arm down. Here's the key: the person that's pushing down must tell you which kind of presentation you are thinking about—a good one or poor one.

We paired and followed Brad's instructions. We were impressed how obvious it was. Brad had demonstrated the importance of our thoughts before we present. We accepted the fact that the quality of our thinking is a key factor because thoughts are real forces.

Now that you know the power of thoughts, use them to your advantage. If you consider the world of sport, every outstanding athlete does some sort of mental preparation. Some athletes use visualizations or mental rehearsal, some use prayer, and others psyche themselves up. What we must do as presenters is find a way to arouse the right emotions for the presentation we are about to do.

THREE ELEMENTS OF CONFIDENCE

Here is a simple way to manage your emotions before a presentation and help to put you in the right space before you speak. First of all, we are going to learn this confidence-generating pattern as a technique, and then we can consider how to use the technique in more of a tailored, subtle way.

This pattern is called "Me, Content, Audience" because it's about you, your content, and your audience. These three variables are the things you need to get juiced up.

ME, CONTENT, AUDIENCE EXERCISE

What would you say if I told you I knew a way for you to be actually, deeply confident before every presentation you give? Here is an exercise we can all do now and take away with us and use before we do any presentation. It will help you find confidence when you need it most!

Brad asked for volunteer who gets a case of nerves at the thought of giving a presentation. Amanda raised her hand and said, "I really struggle with confidence before giving a presentation."

Audience

How do I feel when I really know my audience wants me to deliver a great presentation?

How do I stand when I know they want me to be confident?

How do I breathe when I know they are engaged with me?

Content

How do I feel when I really know my content?

How do I stand when I really know my content?

How do I breathe when I really know my content?

Me

How do I feel when I give my best presentation?

How do I stand when I deliver my best presentation?

How do I breathe when I deliver my best presentation?

"Now, rather than try to explain this to you, I'll just show you how it works," Brad said, pointing to Amanda. *"Amanda, have you got a presentation coming up or a piece of training?" She said that she did. "Good, come up here and stand on this first spot here, just in front of the circle labeled Me."*

ME

Amanda stood in front of the circle. "Now, close your eyes," Brad said, "and imagine it's time for you to do your presentation, and you're feeling anxious about it. When you present, do you feel anxious sometimes?" She nodded yes.

Doesn't take much to imagine that, right? Now, has there ever been a time when you've given a phenomenal presentation? One when you were just brilliant?

She nodded and smiled, raising her hands in victory.

Excellent. So what I want you to do is to step into the Me circle and bring with you that feeling of being at your best. Breathe as you would if you were being the best possible you. You know the times when you've done your best. Think about those times. Think about how you felt and amplify the feelings inside your own mind—feel them even more.

I saw a visible change come over Amanda. She relaxed, and a wonderful smile spread across her face. Her posture became more open and solid at the same time. Actually, she appeared larger than life, and her body swayed, feeling the joy of shining.

There you go. When you feel that you're in the best possible Me space, next step forward into the other circle on the floor and think about your presentation's content. Now step onto the circle of paper marked Content.

CONTENT

When you did such a good job on your excellent presentation, how well did you know your subject?

"Really well, I nailed it," said Amanda.

"How well?" Brad challenged.

"Perfectly," Amanda replied with great certainty.

Now I want you to reexperience that. *Feel* what it was like to know your content, that time when you actually knew deep down what you were talking about, that it was valuable. How was your confidence?

"Sky high. I was Superwoman."

"Beautiful," Brad said, praising Amanda before turning to the rest of us. *"Notice how solid she is in her stance now?"* It was true, Amanda was filled with confidence.

Now, when you feel great about your performance, take the feelings of Me and Content and step into Audience, the third circle.

AUDIENCE

When you did that past successful presentation, did you know your audience? Keep thinking of them. Did they have friendly faces? Imagine your audience sitting there and looking at you smiling. How does it feel?

"I knew most of them—we all worked for the same organization," said Amanda. *"I smiled back, just like I'm doing now. I loved it."*

"But what if you didn't know the audience?" Brad asked her.

"I would smile at them," said Amanda. *"I'm confident they would smile back."*

"There you go," Brad said. *"So if you were to hold onto the feelings you now have while thinking about an upcoming presentation, how do you think it would go?"*

"I feel absolutely confident it would go well!" Amanda said.

"Each of you," Brad said, addressing all of us, *"can do the same thing and step onto the stage with absolute confidence and it will be genuine and truthful. Amanda, thank you for trusting me and allowing the group to see this exercise."* She sat back down.

CHAINING STATES

What we just did is called chaining states. That means we are building a series of positive, resourceful emotions and then amplifying and stacking them on top of each other. This is an incredibly effective process because as we build upon these positive emotions and increase them, they eventually overpower any feelings of concern or worry.

Start with Me because you can be certain about yourself, even if you're less certain about Content and Audience. For me, I just feel it's my job to engage my audience. I say to myself, that's why I'm here and that's why I'm doing this presentation.

You may say that you've never felt confident about presenting. Don't let that concern you. Just imagine that you are confident when presenting. Notice how that feels. Maybe you know someone who is an extremely confident presenter. How does that presenter stand when he presents? Try to stand the same way.

AS IF EXERCISE

When I ask someone to stand like a confident presenter, it's an "as if" technique, which means if you don't know what to do, just act as if you do! It may sound strange and insincere, but *your physiology affects your brain and thoughts*. If the body is confident, your thinking will be confident too, and because of that, you'll find the answer.

Here are the steps to the exercise.

1. Lay out on the floor in front of you three signs labeled:
    a. Me
    b. Content
    c. Audience
2. Stand before the first label—Me—and think of a time (real or imagined) when you did a great presentation. Go back to that time and feel what it was like to you. Amplify those feelings.
3. Once you have those positive feelings, step into the space labeled Me. Amplify those feelings even more. Notice how it felt when you did a wonderful presentation. Once you have all those feelings running through you, step into the space labeled Content.

4. When you did that great presentation, how well did you know your content? How does it feel when you are totally prepared and know your content inside out? How does it feel to be an authority on the presentation you're giving? Amplify those feelings even more.

5. Step into the Audience space. When you think of the people you're presenting to, imagine them looking at you and smiling, nodding and soaking up your presentation. Notice how you feel when you imagine this. Amplify those feelings even more.

6. Take all those positive feelings and just stand with them, noticing how it feels to be confident about yourself, your content, and your audience.

BANG

Be the chess player, not the chess piece.

FREQUENTLY ASKED QUESTIONS

Q. What is the advantage in emphasizing being bigger than life itself?

A. Audiences seldom tolerate wimps. Whatever it is you have to say, audiences want to be engaged during your presentation. Positioning yourself and owning the stage is important. If what you have to present is important, show it and shine while you are sharing it. Go and look at www.ted.com. You'll discover many ways presenters use to put more of themselves into their talks. Learning to put more of *you* into your talk, interview, or presentation has great strategic importance and value.

Q. Can a not-so-confident presenter really acquire confidence? Is confidence really trainable?

A. Yes, absolutely. When babies first learn to walk, their first steps are tentative and they fall down a lot. When youngsters first learn to ride a bicycle, they aren't filled with confidence. But once they get the hang of it, they're speeding around all over the place. Confidence in presenting is also learned. Very few presenters are naturals. Confidence takes practice. Soon you'll be able to project confidence, which your audiences will greatly enjoy. As I've said, audiences hate arrogance and cockiness, but they love genuine confidence.

Q. The Not Me space interests me. Are you suggesting that in order to expand my comfort zone, I should do the "Count to 10" exercise?

A. If that's what it takes and more. Remember that I'm talking about a whole range of physiology: voice, gestures, posture, and emotions. I'm encouraging you to decode what I call your Not Me zone. Instead, work on expanding your Me zone and learn to incorporate all kind of actions that can enhance your presenting, such as bigger gestures, wider range of voice qualities, and using silence and being comfortable with it. Your audience will appreciate seeing more of an expanded version of you.

Q. **So you're encouraging me to be memorable?**

A. Why not? Depending on how much practice you put into presenting, you can become a wonderful presenter. Analogies exist in athletics: many of the Olympic gold winners got there by devoting hours and hours of practice to their events and by using many coaches. In presenting, expand your Me space and narrow your Not Me zone. Try it, you'll like it.

Q. **I've never thought about thoughts being real forces. So getting into a great state is another important thing?**

A. Yes. That means if you want to give a great presentation, you have to be in the right state. You have several options. Two of the most powerful options are: (1) manage your physiology—stand and breathe in a confident way, make some assertive gestures, psyche up just like an athlete does; and (2) manage the quality of your thoughts—think of times when you have succeeded in the past, develop a positive mantra. Anthony Robbins (www.tonyrobbins.com) has an incantation he has used for the last twenty years, and before *every* presentation he says to himself repeatedly "I now command my unconscious mind to do whatever it takes to give me the passion, humor, brevity to empower the people I am blessed to speak with to make the positive choices in their life for their positive good." I prefer you work on both. It's easy to acquire at a conceptual level, but they can be challenging when it comes to the point when you're about to walk on stage or stand up before an interview panel. Practice, practice, practice.

CHAPTER 4

FOCUS YOUR MESSAGE

People ignore design that ignores people.

—FRANK CHIMERO

DON'T REHASH

Eighty percent of all presentations are a rehash—meaning, we cut and paste from previous presentations we have either done or seen. Sound familiar?

It did sound similar. I was guilty of having taken material directly from other presentations. After all, if it had worked for one person, why shouldn't it work for me?

The reason most presenters reuse old material is because it works—it's easy and takes little effort. Sure, they may update the presentation, change a few pictures, change a few facts, substitute current statistics, or drop in a new logo, but essentially, they design a presentation in *hindsight*. That means they look at their presentation goal and look at what they've done in the past to fill the need. But this is simply a survive tactic.

Here's a rule of thumb: The only way to release the real you is for you to create your own presentations. In other words, focus your message.

FOCUSING YOUR MESSAGE

I'm going to break down the process of focusing your message into three chunks: GAP (goal, audience, points), 4MAT, and design musts. When used properly, the whole presentation design process becomes easy—even fun. Let's have a look at a visual diagram of the whole design process so that you can see how it all fits together.

Before you can start down the path to creating a great presentation, you have to know where you are headed. It starts with GAP.

GOAL, AUDIENCE, POINTS

First, ask three questions. What is your goal? Who is your audience? What are the main points of your presentation? Without the right answers to these questions, it's nearly impossible to create an excellent presentation. It's like trying to provide answers without knowing the questions. I use the acronym GAP so that I can focus on why I'm presenting in the first place.

G is for goal. What do I want to have happen? What is the best outcome for me?

A is for audience. Who will be attending?

P is for points. What are your key points?

If you have clear answers to these questions, you will find the process of putting your presentation together much easier and faster. Let's look at GAP more closely.

WHAT IS YOUR GOAL?

What is your goal? Are you there to teach, sell, persuade, or what exactly? What is your desired outcome? What is it that you want, specifically? Write it down. Look at what you wrote. Take a step back and ask yourself this question: If this happens as a result of my presentation will I dance a jig? Or sing a song?

At this point, Brad actually started to do a lively dance and sang a refrain from a famous musical for the class. Wow, I'd like to feel like that at the end of a presentation.

If not, then you need to rethink your goal. But make sure you do this right. There are goals, and there are nongoals that masquerade as goals. An example of a nongoal would be "to teach the class about safety in the workplace." That isn't an outcome. I get bored just saying it. What would be something more like a goal or an outcome?

Brad looked at us expectantly, and people started calling out suggestions: Reduce workplace accidents by 50 percent. Cut down rolling office chair accidents to three per month.

Reducing workplace accidents is an outcome that is an example of a real goal. And cutting down rolling office chair accidents to three per month is also a goal.

WHO IS YOUR AUDIENCE?

Sometimes it's easy to describe who will be in an audience; at other times it's a bit trickier. You may be making a presentation to a team within your company that you meet with regularly. You know them well, and they know you.

On the other hand, you may be making a presentation to a group of people whom you don't know. It may be a collection of individuals with different backgrounds and various levels of knowledge and experience, and you may be unsure of their expectations. Then you will want to tailor your presentation to a certain target audience, even if you have to estimate the details. It basically comes down to three things:

1. What do they care about?
2. What do they know?
3. What do they *not* know?

If you can answer those three questions well—and I really mean well—then you are in a decent position to continue.

WHAT ARE YOUR POINTS?

Imagine that you've been trying to explain an important thing to a good friend, but the subject is complex and your explanation is taking a long time. Your friend gets impatient and says, "OK, OK. I get all of that, but what's your point?"

What do you say? How will you handle this? Do you start at the beginning and go through all of the details again, or do you distill it down to just one or two sentences? If you want to keep that friend, you'd better be brief. Just cut to the chase and state the important message that is at the core of your long explanation.

So before you start creating your presentation, have a clear idea of your main point—or key points, the key message, the message that the audience must get for your presentation to succeed.

4MAT: DIFFERENT LEARNING STYLES

People learn in different ways. Have you ever noticed that some people prefer facts and figures more than motivational messages, and some people love processes and strategies while others prefer "just doing it"? That's because we all have different learning styles. When you present, do you take this into account?

Too often, when we experience presentations, we find the presentation is in one mode. This is the single biggest missed opportunity facing everyone who has to develop a presentation.

I have a left arm and a right arm. It just so happens that I'm more dominant in my right arm. It's the same with learning. We have different ways we learn, and throughout our education, we have preferences in our learning styles. I believe that we should be aware of them.

Each person in your audience has his or her own learning style and relies on it. Based on those preferences, your presentations should appeal to everybody in the audience. However, what I find is that a lot of presenters present using only one or two learning styles, which emanate from their own personal preferences and strengths. And if they happen to use another style, it's through chance not through design. I encourage you to be purposeful in your presentation design, so that everyone in the audience feels as though you are speaking to him or her. I'm going to show you a way to do that. It's very quick and—even better—it makes your presentation more balanced and useful. The method is called 4MAT.

CRACKING THE CODE

There are many types of learning models in the business world, but there is one model that I love using for a few different reasons:

1. It's easy to understand and quick to apply.
2. It drastically decreases presentation design time.
3. You develop rapport with the whole audience.
4. People get a complete story.

Plus, it breaks the age-old habit of designing presentations in PowerPoint. Remember that PowerPoint is a presentation medium, *not* a design tool.

Bernice McCarthy originated 4MAT.[1] Her book is titled *Teaching Around the 4MAT Cycle: Designing Instruction for Diverse Learners with Diverse Learning Styles.* This learning model says that there are four different types of learners who all have different needs that must be addressed in order for them to stay engaged.

---

1 **Managing Learning Styles**
McCarthy, Bernice, and Dennis McCarthy. *Teaching Around the 4MAT Cycle: Designing Instruction for Diverse Learners with Diverse Learning Styles.* Thousand Oaks, CA: Corwin Press, 2005.

TYPE 1. WHY LEARNERS

The key word for a why learner is *relevance*. Right from the start, this learner is thinking, Why is this important to me? If, as a presenter, I make that point, if I create the relevance upfront, what am I going to get from them? Their attention. Now don't get me wrong, everyone needs a why. But why learners need it right from the beginning, otherwise you will quickly lose them.

For instance, if a type 1 learner is learning a new sales process, as soon as you can present the reason *why* it's good to learn the new sales process and its relevance to them. You will also engage them emotionally—early.

Why learners want to know why something is worth doing: Why would we need to know this stuff? Why bother to use it? They like to explore the reasons for taking action before actually doing so.

In fact, any of us with children know that the first question they ever use to drive us insane is why. I can still hear my son sitting in the back of the car saying, "Daddy, Why is the sky blue? Why do my fingers fit into my mouth? Why do the dogs bark? Why…"

TYPE 2. WHAT LEARNERS

Type 2 learners learn best when you give them the information verbally, whether you say it or put it on paper. In presentations and trainings, learners are happiest when there is so much information that they're frantically taking notes, and they can't write fast enough to keep up.

We laughed as Brad mimed the frenzied scribbling of a satisfied what learner, his face suddenly aglow with delight as he whipped his head up and down, looking from his imaginary notes to his imaginary presenter as if nodding.

The criteria of a good presentation for what learners is having plenty of handouts. Provide masses of facts, figures, and statistics. The value of your presentation lies in the thickness of the handouts. I'm not kidding! Learning is all about content. They need the facts, the figures, all the stuff that relates to everything inside their what question. For example, if you are talking about a toy, they want facts about the toy: what it does, its appeal to certain demographics, and its specifications—in detail.

TYPE 3. HOW LEARNERS

Type 3 is the how learners. *How* people learn best by doing. They aren't too bothered about the theory or the reasons; they're just, "Let me at it. Let me try it!" They first want to try things out and get the feel of things. For example, when how people first get their hands on a computer, they just start clicking on anything to see what happens.

As a presenter, you have a coaching role for these learners. Get them to try something, get their feedback on what they did, and then coach them on what they could be doing better. This helps them understand the concept you're sharing better.

TYPE 4. IF LEARNERS

Finally, there are the type 4 learners, the *what if* learners. In general, these people will be considering the consequences of making changes to the structure of your proposal, the consequences of doing it in another context, and any possible repercussions on them—they seldom stick to your guidelines. It is almost as if they are testing the boundaries: finding out where they are, where they could go, and what is possible.

STAR TREK

Think back to your childhood and school. From what types of teachers did you get the best results? And notice I said *teachers* not subjects. Subjects do matter, but only a few teachers generally affected your comprehension and results more than your love of the subject.

Have you ever watched the original *Star Trek* television series? The characters in *Star Trek* are great examples of the learning styles. For example, consider this:

- Captain Kirk was a type 4 learner, an *if* learner. He wants to explore and test the boundaries of the universe.
- Mr. Spock was a type 2 learner, a *what* learner. Unless it was logical, it made no sense.
- Dr. McCoy was a type 1, a *why* learner always looking for reasons. He always asked, "Why are we going to this planet, Jim?"
- Scotty was a type 3 learner, the *how* learner. He wasn't happy unless he had something to fix.

DOCTORS AND PATIENTS

Here's another example of different learning styles. When you go to the doctor this is usually what you want to know:

TYPE 1. WHY LEARNERS

➤ Why am I ill?

➤ Why did this happen?

TYPE 2. WHAT LEARNERS

➤ What is wrong with me?

➤ Tell me about this disease.

TYPE 3. HOW LEARNERS

➤ How did this happen to me?

➤ How are you going to get me better?

TYPE 4. WHAT IF LEARNERS

➤ What if your diagnosis is wrong?

➤ What will happen if I don't treat this. Will it drop off?!

ASSESS YOUR LEARNING STYLE

To get an idea about your own personal learning preference, below is a short profile questionnaire in the form of a table. It'll give a sense of how you learn and what preferences you have.

4MAT SELF-ASSESSMENT

Here is a scoring formula I want you to use.

4—most like you
3—often like you
2—sometimes like you
1—least like you

In the table below, plot your preferences based on the 1–4 scoring allocation. Once you have filled out the table, add the column scores up and put the totals in the boxes in the bottom row. After totaling the columns, transfer your scores to the bottom of the graph and plot them on the vertical axis.

Here's an example:

Meaning	Knowing the facts	Testing theories	Risk Taker
4	2	1	3

49

Meaning	Knowing the facts	Testing theories	Risk Taker
Relevance	Clearly defined goals	Practice	Dynamic
Imagination	Analysis	Problem Solving	Future Opportunities
Need Reason	Logic	Hands-on technique	Self-discovery
Interested	Experts	Demonstrate	Putting new spin on things
Connect with idea	Concepts	Common sense	Intuition
Listening	Observing	Experimenting	Modifying
Speaking	Proof	Manipulating	Adapting
Interacting	Classifying	Improving	Problem anticipation
Brainstorming	Theorizing	Tinkering	Creating
Total	Total	Total	Total

4MAT Scores by Type of Learner

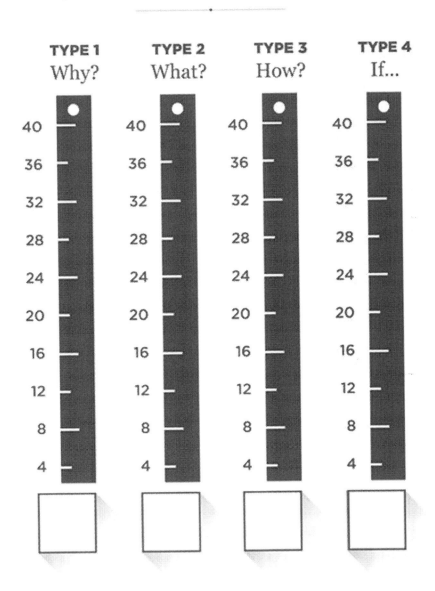

Have you finished? Are you surprised by your results?

Your scores indicate your learning preferences. Often I find people present content with a bias toward their owning learning style. What that means is if your strength is in being a type 2 (what) learner you will most likely deliver your presentation focusing on what messaging. The same is true with the other styles. Our goal must be to land on all four learning styles if we are presenting to a group of people. That means people will have a *whole* learning experience.

Now that you understand what the 4MAT is and why it's so important in helping people get the most of your presentation, do you think it's time we started to apply it?

At that everyone realized that Brad not only knows this stuff, he was teaching us the 4MAT by using the 4MAT. And it made learning feel natural. I was a bit concerned that while it looked easy, I wasn't too sure that I'd be able to do it without a lot of practice.

CREATING A PRESENTATION USING 4MAT

Let's do an exercise so that you can see how easy and effective using the 4MAT is for presentation design. Let's suppose that you need to plan a presentation introducing a commercial community to Performance Management. We'll work through the cycle starting with type 1 learners and ending with type 4 learners.

Imagine for a moment we will be speaking to an audience 150 people who represent the middle tier of an organization. Let's develop a type 1 learner point of view. *Why* is performance management important to these managers? Here are some possible answers.

- Help us develop our employees.
- Help us be more consistent at reward and recognition with employees.
- Identify performance issues before they become a big problem.

Now answer the *what* about performance management for type 2 learners. For example, what is performance management?

- It's a process and tool set that supports team members in their personal and career development by communicating the steps they need to take to progress.
- It defines performance requirements and activity for one's self, team members, and managers.
- It involves the promoting, learning, and development of others to support ongoing and future business improvements.

Now consider the type 3 learner. *How* do you do performance management? How would you focus your presentation for these folks? What solutions do you have for these learners.

- Team and individual performance standards will be clearly communicated, and the reasons for them will be explained in order to gain commitment.
- Specific performance management tools, processes, and training will be offered, allowing you an easier adoption process.
- Address performance below target and identify development targets giving specific positive or developmental feedback.

Now it's time to think about the type 4 learner. What are the consequences for the organization of getting performance management right?

- If we implement performance management, we'll have a more motivated and engaged workforce.
- If people adopt performance management, they will know what is expected of them.

- If we adopt performance management, we'll have a much more capable workforce and organization.

So there you have it. In less than five minutes what have we done? We've structured the flow and content to a presentation. No, easy. But, you may be asking yourself, surely there's more to it just filling boxes.

You bet there is, but what we've done here is mapped out some content in a seamless flow. Now we need to craft a story with the content. Here's a series of prompts that will help you create your content.

STORY BOARDING: QUICK SPEECH PLANNER

1. Why would I want to know about this?

Why would I want to hear about this particular topic you are talking about? What's in it for me? Why is it important for me to know about this? What benefit is there for me getting the information you are going to tell me?

2. What is this all about?

What is the information? What are the facts? What are the essential details that I need to be aware of? What do I need to know about this so I can understand, and make sense of what you are talking about?

3. How will it work for me?

How can I use it? What is the process for my using this? How am I actually going to do it? How can I use this right now? How can I use this information you are giving me in a practical sense? How do I implement these ideas?

4. What if I do use it?

What would happen as a result of my doing what you are saying? What are the consequences of using it, what are the consequences of not using it? What are the future possibilities of continuing to use it?

DESIGN MUSTS

If you can't explain it simply,
you don't understand it well enough.

—ALBERT EINSTEIN

Now that you've defined your GAP created your 4MAT plan, it's time to move on to actually designing the presentation.

There used to be an absence of great design tools. Now there is a plethora of design tools with hundreds of features, so many that they often ruin otherwise good presentations. I've footnoted a few tools and resources for you. But there is good news: I'll share with you some tools, processes, and techniques that will change forever the way you design your presentations. Designing will become easier, more thorough, and much more enjoyable when it comes to formatting your next presentation.

---

2 **Help with Slides**

Duarte, Nancy. *slide:ology: The Art and Science of Creating Great Presentations.* Sebastopol, CA: O'Reilly Media, 2008. Insights into creating more engaging graphics.

Reynolds, Garr. *Presentation Zen: Simple Ideas on Presentation Design and Delivery.* Berkeley, CA: New Riders Press, 2008. Great advice for simplifying your slides to their essence.

Tufte, Edward R. *Envisioning Information.* Cheshire, CT: Graphics Press, 1990. The classic reference for displaying data visually.

———. *The Visual Display of Quantitative Information.* 2nd ed. Cheshire, CT: Graphics Press, 2001. The classic reference about the importance and impact of illustrations in understanding complex concepts.

Williams, Robin. *The Non-Designer's Design Book (3rd Edition).* Berkeley, CA: Peachpit Press, 2008. An excellent introduction to the basic principles of good visual design.

DEVELOP A STORYBOARD

The best presenters spend time designing their story by using storyboards. This allows you to see the flow of your presentation and to ensure the presentation runs smoothly and that your story builds and takes people on a fluid journey.

Cliff Atkinson, in his 2005 book *Beyond Bullet Points* smartly states that starting to create your presentation in PowerPoint before you have your key points and logical flow worked out, on paper or a whiteboard, is like a movie director hiring actors and starting to film before there is a script in hand.

He paused to let his point sink in. I found myself picturing the backward movie director on the phone, shopping around for people to hire when he had no idea what his movie was even about.

I usually use a blank space on a wall or a whiteboard to start to storyboard my 4MAT outputs. I find this approach stimulates my creativity a bit more as I said. No software to get in my way, and I can easily see how the flow will go. I draw sample images that I can use to support a particular point, say, a pie chart here, a photo there, perhaps a line graph in this section, and so on. You may be thinking that this is a waste of time: Why not just go into PowerPoint and create your images there so you do not have to do it twice?

The fact is, if I tried to create a storyboard in PowerPoint, it would actually take longer because I would constantly have to go from normal view to slide-sorter view to see the whole picture. This approach to sketch out my ideas and create a rough storyboard really helps solidify and simplify my message in my own head. I then have a far easier time laying out those ideas in PowerPoint.

I usually do not even have to look at the whiteboard when I am in PowerPoint because this storyboard process alone gave a clear visual image of how I want the content to flow. I glance at my notes to remind me of what visuals I thought of using at certain points and then go to iStockphoto.com or to my own library of high-quality stock images to find the perfect image.

THE STORYBOARD METHOD

To create a storyboard, I usually draw four columns divided into four rows (see graphic below). You can draw one of these yourself, or you can print out a version of this template from my online resource (www.PresentNaked.com). It will make your design process quicker, smarter, and clearer—rather than getting tied up with the limitations of your software capability.

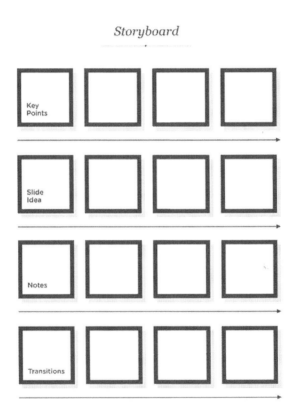

Storyboard

Remember, this is your presenting storyboard. Now, before you begin filling out this chart, write out your GAP (goal, audience, and key points) information and hang it in your workspace. This will keep you focused and guide you as you design your presentation. Don't forget your 4MAT work; you must consider how people learn. The first thing to do is to get a sticky note or a card.

Key Points. The first row is key points. List the main points of your presentation in this row, the flow of your 4MAT structure. You may find there are things that don't add value from your 4MAT brainstorming, and you can discard them. The whole point of a storyboard is to create a *story*.

Slide Ideas. The next row down is slide ideas. Here, you'll jot down any ideas for slides that come to your mind, images that will illustrate the key points you listed above. It would be very easy to create a simple text-based slide, but these days people expect more—something more visual and pleasing to look at as well as to read. If being creative is not your thing when it comes to designing slides, don't fret. Let me give you two references. The best online resource for finding examples of great slide work can be found at www.slideshare.net. It's an amazing resource of slide decks from a variety of contributors. Simply go to the website and search for a topic you are interested in, and you'll find a smorgasbord of great slide decks, a large proportion of which you can download and use as stimulus for your own ideas. If, on the other hand you want to learn how to do it yourself, my go-to recommendation would be to grab any resource created Nancy Duarte. She is gifted at making slide design beautiful and easy to do.

Notes. Next is notes. This is where you'll write down what you're going to say. Remember 4MAT? As you write, remember to keep your why, what, how, and if learners engaged. You will find that this also keep you on track.

Transitions. Finally, at the bottom, you'll come up with transitions, ways to move smoothly from slide to slide, topic to topic. When you know what you'll be talking about during each slide, it will be easier to rearrange them and have them flow together. Throughout this process, you'll want to be working analog, of course. If you're working with paper instead of a whiteboard, then make all your plans on sticky notes and just stick them up in the box where you want to try it out. If you don't like it there, it's easy to just move it somewhere else or get rid of it completely. With all that done, you now have a very tidy presentation design. You also have a flow that will appeal to everyone in the audience in terms of flow and balance of content. With your slides and materials developed, you're ready to go live after a bit of rehearsing!

SLIDE JUNK

Slide skills are an esoteric, dark art for most of us, and I can recommend three leading software firms that produce programs for slide-based presentations.[3]

But in the meantime, I have ten points to guide you and help you avoid what I call slide junk. The overriding principle, as you know by now, is that it is *you* that brings the PowerPoint slides alive, not the computer. So please keep the following in mind as you create your slides:

1. Master the basics and a few signature specialities; your audience will be dearly thankful.
2. Keep it simple. Less is more. If you need lots of data and facts, break it down into clearly visible chunks. Resist the urge to fill in blank spaces. Instead, use handouts to supplement your slides.
3. Where possible don't use bullet points. Be more creative in how you display information. Again, go online and have a look at what the

---

3 **Presentation Software**
PowerPoint, Microsoft (office.microsoft.com/powerpoint/): Some love it, many hate it. Still the overwhelming standard for both Mac & PC.
Keynote, Apple (www.apple.com/iwork/keynote/): Apple's alternative to PowerPoint, part of the iWork suite. Mac only.
Prezi (www.prezi.com): Prezi is a web-based presentation application and storytelling tool that uses a single canvas instead of traditional slides. Free.

experts do. A lot of media agencies showcase their work online. Use their examples as a catalyst for your creations. Have a look at the open source slide website called www.slideshare.net, and look at the top slide decks that have been posted online. I am a big fan of a slide designer on there called Slides that Rock.

4. Sixty to 80 percent of all text can be deleted. Remember that PowerPoint is a display tool to reinforce and highlight your presentation. It should never be a script; that's what handouts are for.

5. Make it a sin to use what I call the "party features" in PowerPoint. They include noisy graphics, spinning letters and objects, word art, clip art, and anything else that may look or sound cheap. It will only remind your audience of other mediocre presentations they have suffered through, and these gimmicks will diminish your otherwise great presentation.

6. Templates. The PowerPoint templates are becoming better, but stick to your company ones or create some unique templates. You can even buy some professional templates for a small fee online. My favorite places to buy templates are www.graphicriver.net and www.envato.com.

7. Colors and fonts. Stay away from all pastels. They work only when the room is pitch black and the projector has strong illumination; otherwise they wash out your presentation. Primary colors are a sure thing. And keep your color theme consistent throughout the presentation. The same rules apply for your font usage.

8. Use professional images. There's nothing worse than seeing images in a presentation with bad resolution, where the image looks blurred. For about the cost of an apple (the fruit variety) you can purchase professional images that add quality and impact to your presentation. I use www.fotolia.com and www.istockphoto.com.

9. Slide quantity. I've never heard anyone say, wow, I really enjoyed your one-hundred-slide presentation. We all like a Goldilocks amount— not too little and not too much. There are no hard-and-fast rules

about how many slides to include. I say use as few as possible—just enough to get your message across. But think about the quantity in conjunction with the time you have allocated to present. I've seen many a presentation where the minutes available directly correlate to the number of slides: twenty minutes equals twenty slides. That's a big no-no. Personally, I apply the rule of three. What time you have, divide it by three as a maximum slide deck.

10. Movie files and sounds. There is an exciting trend to include YouTube clips in presentations now, and it's a great medium. Always choose the best resolution and ensure the sound and pictures work before screening the movie clip.

11. Become familiar with sources that help your preparedness[4]

REHEARSE

I don't think that I've ever seen a presentation that was not improved by rehearsal. That may sound obvious enough, but how many presenters actually rehearse their presentations? Even once—aloud and in front of other people? The only rehearsal most of us do is in the comfort and safety of our own heads! The three main reasons we don't rehearse is pretty obvious when you think about it. We don't rehearse because the presentation generally isn't finished until the day of the presentation, we don't have time to rehearse, and lastly because we are frightened of receiving any constructive feedback.

Rehearsal and feedback is the breakfast, lunch and dinner of champions. It's no different than a singer learning a song or a football player learning a move. In all walks of competitive life, rehearsal takes place. In presentations

---

4 **Where to Look for Presenting Resources**
Slideshare (www.slideshare.net): Slide decks posted on almost any topic from contributors from around the world.
http://neuland.biz and www.pinpoint-facilitation.com: Pinpoint and Graphic Facilitation process and products.

it's a rare experience. The few times I see people rehearse are just before large conferences. However, the rehearsal is usually done to simply run through the presentation, get the cues and timing right, and quality check the content. There is much more to be gained from rehearsals. Some of those benefits are as follows:

- Internalize the content.
- Gain more confidence.
- Build on delivery style.
- Make great refinements.
- Get feedback.

DON'T CRAM

Remember how in school, sometimes, the night before a big paper was due or the night before a final exam, you would stay up all night cramming? Don't. This is the best way to ensure that you will immediately take the short-cut of using a PowerPoint deck that you or someone else created in the past. You won't have the time to rehearse the key points that you really want to get across to the audience. You will tend to use the slides to guide your words rather than using the slides to enhance what you are saying.

The key to all of this is simple. Plan enough time to develop and practice your presentation. Just think of all those people who present so effortlessly or those athletes that make their sport look easy. They make it look easy because they practice, practice, practice. Remember this: what you practice in private gets rewarded in public!

FREQUENTLY ASKED QUESTIONS

Q. With your emphasis on focus, what do I do if some people in the audience don't appear interested early in my presentation?

A. It's not that simple. Presumably, you were invited to present because there is an interest in what you have to say. It may take a while for some people in your audience to accept your findings.

I know of a presenter who faced immediate audience hostility. The presenter stopped, went to visit the group's vice president, who came into the room and explained his goals for the organization and why this presentation was being given and then invited anyone who wanted to leave to come to his office and collect their paycheck. No one left, and the presentation turned into a winning experience for everyone. This is a rare experience. Follow my approach and principles, and you won't get into much trouble; quite the opposite.

Q. How do I know that my topic and the audience's goal are in synch?

A. This is a key question, but most people in your audience are there because they've heard of your topic or about you or both. Most people are inclined to give you a chance. If you're presenting merrily along and people aren't heading for the exits, your topic is probably in alignment with leadership's and the audience's interest. Just keep going.

Q. Won't my focus and message look pretty much like everyone else's?

A. This depends on what you mean by "look like everyone else's." In a sense your presentation should look like others' presentations. Whoever invited is expecting similarity. But your unique opening should create differentiation, and the ways you light up the room, combined with a less-is-more approach to slides, will help you.

Q. **Since competitors present in similar ways, will I really stand out?**

A. Presenters look the same because they don't stand out. Most people struggle to stand out. First, make sure your GAP analysis is correct. Next, remember the likelihood that the room contains four kinds of learners—*why* learners, *what* learners, *how* learners, and those who ask all of the *if* questions while they learn. Then make a great storyboard, using the four rows to help you: key points, slide ideas, notes, and appropriate, clear transitions. Do it well and your message will be focused, coordinated, and filled with clarity.

CHAPTER 5

LET YOURSELF SHINE

Abake babonana bayophinde babonane futhi.
Those of us who have truly seen one another will surely
see one another again.

—ZULU SAYING

Time for you to shine. Time for you to put more of yourself out there. Move beyond the chalk-and-talk techniques of clinical presentations and move into the plus points of your own style. Letting yourself deliver a personal presentation steeped in personal truth is summarized in the famous passage written by Marianne Williamson from *A Return to Love: Reflections on the Principles of a "Course in Miracles."*

> Our deepest fear is not that we are inadequate. Our deepest fear is that we are powerful beyond measure. It is our light, not our darkness, that most frightens us. We ask ourselves, who am I to be brilliant, gorgeous, talented and fabulous? Actually, who are you not to be? You are a child of your God. Your playing small doesn't serve the world. There is nothing enlightened about shrinking so that other people

won't feel insecure around you. And as we let our own light shine, we unconsciously give other people permission to do the same. As we are liberated from our own fear, our presence automatically liberates others.

Nelson Mandela used most of that passage in his inauguration speech back in 1984. If you consider Mr. Mandela as a speaker, you'll notice that those listening to him will hang on his every word. When you try to dissect what makes a powerful, truthful speaker, it's not his or her loudness or other extroverted behaviors. I think it's something much, much deeper. We touched on it when we experienced some of those activities in chapter 2, "Just You." But right now I want to introduce to you a concept you won't find in any other presentation program, and it comes from the heart of South Africa.

SERITI

In the countries of South Africa and Lesotho, there's an indigenous tribe called the Sesotho and they speak about people having *seriti*. Loosely translated, it means your shadow and what image your shadow projects. In the context of a presentation, it's someone whose *seriti* is large enough to fill the room much like Nelson Mandela does. Who else in your experience has a large *seriti*? Some possibilities are: Oprah Winfrey, Bill Clinton, Madonna, Martin Luther King, Winston Churchill.

These are all great names, but they are public figures. Think closer to home. Who, from your own experience, has a *seriti* that impacts you—a person whose presence speaks louder than his or her words?

Everyone—including you and me—has a *seriti*. Some people's *seriti* is transparent, while others have a strong and bright one. How large your shadow is depends on the inner strength of your character. I go to Africa as often as I can; I love Africa. The lesson of *seriti* was explained to me while I sat around a campfire with some of the most wonderful Africans you'll ever get to meet.

One of them said, "Your *seriti* is like the shadow you cast from the flames of this fire and it's reflection in the night. Your *seriti* can be measured by the feeling you leave with people after you leave."

Looking into *seriti* a bit deeper in Sesotho is more complex than the usual English translation of shadow, which combines the possible meanings of *moriti* and *seriti*. Santu Mofokeng is one of South Africa's most celebrated photographers, recognized for his work with the Afrapix collective and on the newspaper *New Nation*. He records a country struggling to come to terms with its past and future. According to Mofokeng, *seriti* can mean anything from aura, presence, dignity, confidence, spirit, essence, status, well-being, and power—power to attract good fortune and to ward off bad luck and disease. And we have heard the expression, "You make your own luck." I encourage you to expand your *seriti*!

SERITI WITH ENERGY

The single biggest differentiator in being a Naked Presenter is the energy you bring to a presentation. Think about the statement I used to start this book (or, for that matter, a seminar): Some people light up the room when they present. When someone lights up the room, that's not simply a consequence of great body language, rich vocal qualities, and effective eye contact. (Don't misunderstand me; those are all essential elements of the appropriate skills of presenting.) But there must be something that occurs at a deeper level—your *seriti* must shine. Your energy must shine through.

Let's have a look at ways that can help you connect with your *seriti*. Don't worry: this is something you can do without feeling embarrassed or weird!

BEFORE YOU BEGIN, START WITH THE RIGHT MIND-SET

For this exercise, find a bit of space where you won't touch anybody or anything and point straight out in front of you. If you right arm is up, turn to your right, if your left arm is up, turn to your left.

We all started turning the way he instructed.

Turn & Point

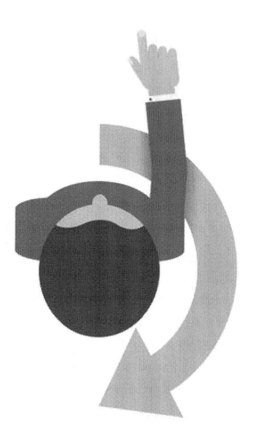

You will be twisting and turning to what I call your soft limit. This is where you naturally stop. You're not putting any unnatural stress on your body. Notice where that place is and then turn back to where you started from.

First, close your eyes and imagine yourself going round to that place that you twisted to. You don't need to move; just go there in your imagination. Now go a second time in your own mind, but go farther still—and you can because it's your imagination. Twist and go farther than that. Farther. Now come back to center.

Brad's tone grew more intense, and I could tell he was getting to the heart of this exercise.

Do this one more time, but because it's your imagination, go round a full 360 degrees. Feel what it's like in your imagination that you can go that far. Now, open your eyes, put your arm up if it's not already up, and turn freely until you stop. See how far you turned this time.

I did as he told me, and I was surprised to see that I had turned much farther. Other people in the class voiced their surprise as well.

You went much farther that time, didn't you? How did that happen? What created that?

Thought? someone said.

Here's the thing, though, it doesn't even have to be a belief, because you didn't believe you could do that, could you? A 360? Of course not. We didn't really believe we could do the 360, but we went so much farther anyway. You don't even have to believe it for it to work.

Now, imagine this, let's apply this to presenting. You walk into a room, see a lot of faces, and they're not that friendly. You think, "I don't want to be here." What's that going to do to your presentation, potentially? Destroy it.

Some of the best speeches or presentations are done in nonperfect conditions. That's what makes them the best: because the presenter stood up and went beyond what was required.

CHANGING YOUR INTERNAL STATE

If you want to change your internal state, you've either got to change your internal thoughts, or change your physiology. The quickest way is to change your physiology. What do I mean? What do you think? If you change your posture and body language, you can change your attitude. To get yourself into a better state, move around, walk around, loosen up.

Give yourself the best chance of success by creating the most beneficial mind-set *before* you start speaking. Remember, thoughts *are* real forces.

YOUR THREE NATURAL GIFTS

They are true gifts and they are expandable:

- Your energy
- Your physiology
- Your voice

You can learn to build and expand your three natural gifts. Here's a story that illustrates my point regarding energy.

I have a wonderful friend called Jeff Nicholson. He's an actor who is currently performing in the London production of the musical *Les Miserables*. He gets out onstage and performs the musical eight times a week. If you've never seen the production, it's based on novelist Victor Hugo's famous account of a cul-de-sac revolution in France back in 1815. It's a deeply moving and highly energized production. I've asked Jeff on many occasions how does he always seem so fresh when he's performing? His answer is always consistent. "Even though this might be the two-hundredth time I've done the show, to the paying audience, it's their first performance. That means *I've got to 'show up' in every performance because the audience knows when you're not on your game.* How I perform affects how *they* feel."

The same applies to us when we present, whether it's our first presentation or the twentieth time we've made the same speech. Our energy directly influences how the audience feels.

Here's how I think about it. What do I want my audience feeling? Speaking for myself, whatever answer I decide, I know I must be in that emotional state when I present. If I want people to be fired up about what I'm presenting, I've got to be fired up. If I want them to believe my message, I must deliver it in a

70

way filled with sureness and with proof. I'm continually amazed at the large number of presenters who fail to make this connection.

I often coach people in a live environment, meaning they do a presentation in front of an audience and afterward we discuss how it went. Supposing I ask the presenter what he thought the mood of the group was and how he felt the audience received his presentation, and he says, "Their response was a bit flat. They didn't seem too interested or enthusiastic." I then ask, "How was your mood?" He may say that he was tired or found the presentation hard work. When I point out that the mood of the group was in rapport with him, the presenter usually reacts with genuine surprise.

When a presentation goes flat, you may wonder, was it your mood that set the tone, or did the audience bring you down? The answer is irrelevant. *You*, the presenter, always set the tone, tempo, and mood of the group. You are the mood monitor of the room; you must be the lighthouse of energy that fills the room. If you do that, all will follow!

YOU ARE THE PRESENTATION

When presenting, this is my advice: *Be you plus 30 percent.* That's it. It means be normal and natural, just do things bigger. I have no hard-and-fast rules about body language because it's a completely subjective experience. Take for instance, crossing your arms when you present. How many think if I did that I'm being defensive at this moment in time.

No hands went up.

See, no one. Does that make crossing your arms OK? Yes and no.

MEANING

Here's the killer distinction I learned through Neuro Linguistic Programming (NLP): nothing has any meaning *except the meaning I give it*. For instance, if someone in the audience thinks I'm being defensive, guess what? They're right! If that's the case, I need to be aware of the things that

71

enhance my impact or credibility with my audience. Equally I need to be aware of the things that will hinder or harm my credibility and impact.

THE YOU PLUS 30 PERCENT PRINCIPLE

Brad asked for a volunteer to join him, someone who gesticulates a lot when they talk, meaning they use their hands a lot.

Paula went up to the front of the room. Brad asked her to describe to us all how she cooked her favorite meal. True to form, she used lots of gestures that were painting pictures of how she cooked.

Brad turned to us and said, "She looks very natural, doesn't she? Who's now interested in tasting what she just described?"

We all raised our hands, mostly in support of Paula.

He then said to Paula, "Tell us once more, but this time exaggerate your gestures—make them twice as big as before. It may feel strange, but pretend it's normal."

Paula went through her cooking description once again, but this time she used exaggerated gestures.

Afterward, Brad asked, "How did that feel, Paula?"

"A little weird," she said. "It felt wrong."

Brad turned to the rest of us and asked, "What did that look like and how did Paula make you feel?"

I said, Paula made me feel even hungrier. The group laughed and agreed. But I wasn't joking. Her larger-than-life gestures looked completely normal. If anything, they had more impact on us.

Increasing the size of your gestures in a presentation increases the impact. Think of it like turning up the volume of your radio. If you were alone listening to the radio, you'd have the volume turned to a normal level; however, if you want the sound to fill the room, you'd turn up the volume. The same goes with your gestures. But it may feel really strange to begin with—or even feel wrong. If that's the case, don't worry. Just remember it's the sign of you entering the Not Me space.

Here is an example of a gesture in a conversational' style.

The same gesture needs to become larger to have an impact with an audience.

Improving your body language and voice is common sense when you are working on enhancing your presentation style. Most things can be remedied quickly. The challenging part is ensuring that you change the habit. The best way to change a habit is through doing more presentations and rehearsals.

FOUNDATIONAL PRINCIPLES

LOOSEN UP

Imagine it's Sunday afternoon, and you're at my place for a BBQ. There is a group of eight of us standing around, and you're telling us about a holiday you've just had. Chances are you're relaxed and in a state of flow. If you can remember that feeling or something similar, that's the loose feeling you want when you present. Remember to loosen up.

NOTICING

How many presenters will notice coughing or other forms of audience disengagement? More importantly, how many will do something about it? The truth is, most presenters don't notice it, and if they do, they don't do anything about it.

One way to take care of it is to find some way to include the audience members who are disengaging. For example, I could be talking to one part of a room because a question came from that side of the room, but through my expanded vision I notice the people in the opposite part of the room are starting to shift around in their seats. That's when I readjust and stand in such a way that I include the other side of the room in the conversation. That part of the room unconsciously feels included once again. It's just a little skill that makes a major, *major* difference. By practicing this exercise you get two big wins:

1. You get in touch with and expand your *seriti*—your presence begins to fill the room.
2. You expand your conscious awareness within the room, allowing you to notice and work with the dynamics within the room.

PAUSES AND SILENCE

There's a wonderful South African named Ian Thomas. He travels the world, and he talks about prides of lions. He says we can take the analogy of a pride of lions and compare them to successful teams. Teams need the same principles as a pride of lions to be successful. Ian was a South African bush ranger, and he tells stories about the life and struggles of a pride of lions.

In a presentation I did with him not too long ago, the stage was enormous; it was about fifty feet across.

Brad started walking to the other side of the room and stopped at the far end.

Ian talked about what the lions are doing on this side of the stage.

Brad calmly paced back to the other side of the room.

Then he stopped and he talked about it from the point of view of the zebras over here, and he had a good five-second gap of speech between here and there, like you observed. But he was so congruent with it, that the audience hung on his every word. His silences were so powerful, they were deafening.

I began to understand how pausing in the right place could have a great deal of impact in a presentation. So, too, did the other attendees.

He didn't go "excuse me," and he didn't muddle it up. There's no leakage in what he does. For those who are wondering what leak means in this context, it means he doesn't say the random thoughts that occur in his mind. Sometimes it's like we have two voices in our heads when we present. One voice is what the audience hears. The other is our private voice, telling us what to do, say, and be frightened of. Leaking happens when we let the audience hear both voices. Leakage lowers your ability to be congruent, meaningful, and impactful. What you want is silent impact.

Here's a personal story. When my dad died, and I spoke at his funeral. It was the hardest thing I've ever done, the absolute hardest thing without a fraction of a doubt. That was where the lessons I'm talking about in this book really made the difference, and had I not known what I did, I probably would have been a complete mess. But don't get me wrong, there's nothing wrong with being a complete mess from time to time!

I had a fear I was going to struggle to get my words out because of my emotions. So before the service, I placed my journal with my speech behind the pulpit in the church. When it was my turn to share my thoughts about my father, I walked up to the pulpit, and felt an attack of involuntary lip jitters coming on. My back was to the congregation. The priest who was conducting the service was sitting right in front of me, and he gave me that knowing look of love and compassion. His look gave me permission to be still, to be silent, and to gather myself for one of the most important speeches of my life.

For a long moment, Brad said nothing, the room alert with the power of his silence.

I didn't apologize. I said nothing and took my time. I took my time to place my journal on the pulpit, put the book down, and open to the right page. I felt my eyes were misting up again. I took a very big, grounding breath to help get centered. And do you know what? No one thought that silence was horrible. The worst thing for me to have done would have been to go, "Oh, sorry, I'm really upset." Just be you, because people will accept you as you are, and we don't have to invent reasons for not being us.

PERSONAL HYGIENE MATTERS

This is a sensitive topic, but I must mention it. Last weekend I sat through about six presentations at a well-known university and one presenter had the worst nervous sweat rings under his arms. Although being overwhelmed giving a presentation and sweating can't be helped, there are thing you can do that will stop people noticing your anxiety.

- Use a good deodorant.
- Wear an undershirt underneath your shirt.
- Wear colors that does not show you are sweating.
- Wear a jacket or sweater over your shirt.

Recently, I was sitting at the back of a conference room, watching a man deliver a presentation. He wasn't showing any sign of nerves during his presentation, but his sweat-drenched shirt made his pitch less effective. Discussing this type of thing can be embarrassing, but we owe it to colleagues to help them to present successfully.

THE PRESENTATION SPACE

Let's examine the space in which we must present. The best presenters know how to be at one with the space they are presenting in. Presenters not at ease with their space can look like a rabbit caught in the headlights. Audiences easily pick up on it.

The class laughed as Brad demonstrated, his face becoming the picture of bewildered fear, his eyes enormous. I could almost see the long, furry ears of a rabbit drooping from his head.

Presenters that shine can make the space they find themselves in feel like home. It's something we must learn, and when we do, it puts the audience at ease as well.

In the early 1990s I sold tickets to Anthony Robbins's seminars. I had to present a forty-five minute seminar that had to convince my audiences to buy tickets to one of Tony's programs. My presentations took place in areas never meant for presentations: it was awful—from open-plan offices to smoking rooms and office reception areas. You soon learn to use your space well and not get flustered or distracted by phones ringing, interruptions, and, most importantly, ridiculous presentation spaces.

Here are a few things to think about when working in a traditional space.

LIGHTS

First, if you are on a stage that has spotlights, *stay in the light*. If you're not used to standing with a spotlight on you, then rehearse with one. Otherwise you might find yourself trying to step out of the light because it's too bright for you. Just recently I watched a very proficient actor present, and he had not marked out where the spotlights focused on stage; consequently, he continuously walked in and out of the light. It was almost a case of now you see him, now you don't. When you do rehearse, ask someone to give you feedback about staying in the spotlight. It can make or break your impact.

THE STAGE ITSELF

Using a stage and its space is a workshop all on its own. You only have to go to the theater and watch how a professional uses space. Here are some keys.

Take your time when approaching the stage; don't be in a rush. Center yourself before you go onstage so you arrive centered. Doing this will help give you presence, and your audience will feel it.

As you look out at the audience, smile and notice who gives you feedback by smiling back. Use these people as your energizers. When I present to large groups such as Redken of L'Oreal, I home in on people who give me back energy when I smile outward. It keeps you feeling good while you are doing your magic. One thing extra I have noticed about this is that other people tend to feel unconsciously energized because of people around them are smiling. It's like there is a resonance around them. After you finish your presentation, you'll feel energized rather than depleted. The only time I ever feel drained is when I get nothing back from the people I'm presenting to—and yes, it happens. So put your smiles out there and stay focused on where they come back from. Work the room.

PODIUMS

Now, the great debate about podiums is this. Do you stand behind them, do you show you're more modern by standing beside them, or do you completely ignore them and walk the floor? If the only microphone available is attached to the podium, your destiny is sealed. Personally, I don't mind a podium because it can give me more authority through stillness. But avoid a few bad habits that can come from podium-based microphones.

Don't hold the edges of the podium like you're playing a pinball machine. As you reach the podium, put your notes on the top, stay present, take a centering breath, look out to the audience (even if you can't see them because of the spotlight on you), and smile. Then start your presentation and simply act naturally. Shine.

Don't keep referring to your notes. That's the worst thing about having notes: you keep referring to them even though you don't need them. Actors have an expression used during rehearsals called "book down." That means it's time to leave your script in your bag and time to trust that you know the material. At most, I encourage people take a copy of a slide map up with them so they can track their slides as they present. In the current versions of PowerPoint, there is an option in the slide show tab called "Presenter View." Using this view when you present allows you to keep your timing by seeing the next slide; you have a film-strip view of all your slides. It's a long overdue feature of the program.

But if you *do* take notes to the podium, use a technique I like to call "scoop and speak." When you look down at your notes, scoop up a sentence or two, then look back at the audience and continue on with your presentation. This method also works very effectively when you rehearse your presentation. Use your finger to trace your written speech, moving your finger as you speak to help you see where you are in your speech.

Don't turn to face the screen when you are making your point. By all means gesture toward the screen but keep your attention on the audience and stay facing them.

Don't be in a hurry to click through your slides. If you are using a podium, there is a strong chance someone else will be managing your slides. Often it's a technical AV support person. There is a button on the podium you click, and the AV support gets the signal to click onto the next slide. In theory and practice it works very well, until a time delay occurs and you think the signal didn't get through so you click again and then all of a sudden you are a slide ahead of yourself and are caught in limbo land with no way to get back to the slide you want! There are two simple remedies for this.

Slow down for an extra second for the AV support to catch up, and if you are ahead of yourself, just ask the AV team to back up a slide for you.

Most importantly, never panic. Stress only shows on you when you panic, so don't. Just take it in stride, breathe, and stay present. If you do this, I promise your audience will say to you afterward how impressed they were in how professionally you dealt with a potential problem.

MEANINGFUL MOVEMENT

If you're going to move, move with purpose. Don't wander. Walk to a place then stop. Do your business, and then move again. If I were king for a day, I'd have all presenters learn to love not moving, just being still. It adds much more presence to the presentation. Notice I said still—not rigid! If you look at any of the following presenters online, you'll notice how credible they are by just being still: John F. Kennedy, Barack Obama, Martin Luther King, Margaret Thatcher, Al Gore.

Sure, they'll move around, but when they are making a point, they don't move. Their words, tone, expression, and gestures are what have impact, not walking around a stage.

HANDLING QUESTIONS AND OBJECTIONS

1. Prepare for all possible questions and objections. Spend time thinking about your presentation from an opposing debater's point of view and ask yourself: What do I need more clarity on, what would I challenge?
2. Have a practice session. Nothing beats preparation.
3. Don't waffle. Answer the question succinctly. Don't be afraid to not know the answer. Car park the question and offer to come back to the question later.
4. Involve the audience. Acknowledge the question, restate the question, and ask audience members to share their views.
5. Let people know when you will handle questions.
6. Keep questions on a tight leash. Questions can often be the thing that causes presentations to run over and/or to go off track. Make sure you stay on time.
7. Be nondefensive. Be open and welcoming—even to tough or aggressive questions.
8. Be attentive to the questioner. Be focused on the questioner and actively listen. Once his or her question has been asked, acknowledge the person for the question and restate the question so the whole room hears it.
9. Satisfy the questioner and the rest of the audience. Once you have finished dealing with the question, ask the person who asked the question if that answers his or her inquiry.

10. Check for understanding the quality of what you have said and whether it satisfies the questioner's need.

LENGTH DOESN'T MATTER

Less is almost guaranteed to be more. It's not too often we hear an audience member say, "I wish his presentation went on longer!" In fact, the opposite is probably true.

Dame Ellen MacArthur has some great principles when she's out sailing with limited onboard resources. "Just because a manufacturer has put a perforated line in the kitchen towel doesn't mean that's where I'm going to tear it. I tear the amount I need, which is often less than the tear lines would suggest, which is how I make my kit last for two months at sea."

Let's apply the same sort of thinking to a presentation. Just because you have a thirty-minute slot allocated to your next presentation, do you feel obliged to fill it? I know I do sometimes. Whereas, if you focused hard on the purpose and outcome of your presentation, you'll be amazed at how informative, engaging, and effective you can make it while taking less time. And better still, your audience will thank you for it! The www.ted.com web presentations give presenters an eighteen-minute time slot: it seems to be the perfect length for a presentation.

Challenge yourself with your next presentation. Whatever time you are given, see if you can cut it by a third. I reckon if we all did that, we'd have much better presenters and fewer people suffering with nodding-dog syndrome, pretending to be awake.

THE MASTERS AND DELIVERY

Learn from the masters. There are so many examples of great presenters that we can all go out and watch, whether it's presentations inside our companies, our schools, or our industries or what we see television or via YouTube. On YouTube alone, there are thousands upon thousands of high-quality presentations that we can watch from all over the world.

You can learn a tremendous amount through other people's expertise, allowing you to avoid having to go through the school of hard knocks. Go and dedicate a couple of hours a month and search for great presentations and watch them. For example, go to www.ted.com. Make a note of what makes Ted presenters great. Notice how they move, how they sound, how they connect with the audience. This is an incredibly effective way of learning how to become more confident, proficient, and impactful. You can capture the essence of how they present and build the things that work well into your own style.

Don't get me wrong. I'm not trying to encourage you to go out there and be a Barack Obama, Tony Robbins, or Steve Jobs when you present. I'm asking you to look for the very things that make these people great presenters. It may be that gesture or that specific way that they emphasis a word when they speak. Take that element and add it to your existing natural ability.

SHOW YOUR PASSION

If you're speaking about something and people want to hear what you're talking about, show your energy and passion. Let them know it's something you feel excited about. Passion helps create rapport with the group. Audiences like it when presenters exhibit passion for their topics. Never curb your enthusiasm because of the subject matter. It doesn't matter if you are presenting statistical data or launching a new product. Passion adds power to your words.

OTHER DO'S

Do you plus 30 percent. Expand your natural style by venturing into the Not Me space.

1. Project a clear voice. Learn to project your voice without screaming.

2. Vocal variety. One of the best ways I found to develop my voice and create a high degree of variety when I speak was by reading children's stories. If you read a child a story from a children's book and you read like an adult, they give you pretty quick feedback about your reading skills! I learned that as you read books to children, you take the child on an adventure or journey. When it comes to presenting, we need to know what words emphasize. We need to be able to create variety in our pitch, speed, and tone. Sometimes we need to squeeze the juice out of the words. 3.

4. I expect when people practice and rehearse, they feel uncomfortable at the beginning but that again is just another sign that you're in the Not Me space. You must push through that level of self-critic and act as if you love rehearsing. You'll be amazed how quickly you'll improve when you do this.

5. Use a remote device. There's nothing worse than watching someone fumbling over their keyboard as they tried to advance their slides. Go and make the best investment of thirty dollars you'll ever make in any presentational equipment. Buy a remote device. I personally use a Kingston remote for the simple reason that it's cheap, effective, lightweight, and easy to use. It's a plug-and-play device, which means you just plug the USB into the side of your computer, and it works all by itself.

   The remote device allows you to move around the room without having to stay close to computer. It has an infrared beam you can use to highlight something on the screen. It gives you the freedom to be more natural and to be yourself without having to stand and click through your slides.

6. Treat the audience as family. I'm making one big assumption about this point—that we all love our family! Let's pretend for a moment that we all do. That means when you present, speak to them respectfully,

gracefully, intelligently, and warmly. They've given their time to be in the room to listen to you speak, so treat them with that same sort of grace and with the common care that makes them feel that they are important.

7. Speak intelligently. Avoid buzzwords, jargon, or overly formal language. When you present, be understandable by using good old-fashioned everyday diction. There are no prizes for trying to prove that you have the best command of your language on the planet. In fact it can have the opposite effect. I've noticed that when people use more formal language when they present, they appear uptight and static. At the opposite end of that scale, language can also be too casual and relaxed. Find somewhere in between the two, and you'll be warmly received.

8. Enjoy yourself. Suffering should be an optional activity when it comes to preentations. If you're going to deliver a presentation enjoy it.

SMILE

And finally, here is the *killer skill* that'll put you ahead of 99 percent of all presentations—*smile*. Smile and the whole world smiles with you. How hard is it to smile?

Why, then, do nine-tenths of presenters fail to smile when they present? I mean, smiling should never be an optional activity for most presentations, but it's pretty rare. However, it seems to be one of the most constant bits of feedback I have to give when coaching good people to present. It makes an enormous difference in developing rapport with the group, putting yourself at ease, and setting the tone for your presentation.

Newsreaders don't smile for a reason: they can't show their personal opinions or thoughts. But when we present it's important to show our passion, excitement, and feelings: it can light up the room!

Following are some suggestions to help you remember to smile.

1. If you are using notes, write the word *smile* in a different color pen in the margin at various and appropriate sections in your presentation.
2. If you are presenting to a group you know, ask one or two people to smile at you when you look at them: it'll help you to remember.
3. If you are running a session using flip charts, draw a welcome poster with a big, cheesy smile on it and pin it up where you can readily see it to remind you.

A lot of these tips aren't rocket science; they're easy to do. But that's the problem. If they're easy to do, they're also easy not to do. The simple stuff matters.

DON'TS: HOW TO WEAKEN YOUR STYLE

1. Do any or a combination of the presentation archetypes.
2. Fiddle with things.
3. Stand with your legs crossed (women often do this).
4. Shuffle with your feet.
5. Look out the window.
6. Continually fidget or rub a part of your face or body.
7. Look tortured.
8. Pace around.
9. Squint if the lights are on you.
10. Punctuate every sentence with umm or end every sentence with OK.
11. Use passive language, such as the words *hopefully*, *might*, and *sometimes*.
12. Constantly clear your throat.

This list should give you a good idea of how to distract and not impress your valuable audience!

FREQUENTLY ASKED QUESTIONS

Q. Should we take your story of *seriti* seriously?

A. Why not? It is particularly useful for presenters. If you recall, the Sotho people in Africa refer to one's *seriti* or the shadow you cast. Presenters cast this shadow in their presentations. Combine it with energy, and it results in amazing impacts on your audience. It is unique to you, and no two are alike. I think it's a fitting metaphor.

Q. I can see that my three gifts—my energy, physiology, and voice— really are expandable. But can I sustain them through a whole presentation?

A. The short answer is absolutely yes. Do you remember the story of my friend Jeff Nicholson, the actor in London? Remember Jeff's answer to my question about how he manages to always seem so fresh when he's performing: *"I've got to 'show up' in every performance because the audience knows when you're not on your game.* How I perform affects how *they* feel."

Q. Are you pinpointing physiology when you say "Be you plus 30 percent"?

A. Physiology can do a lot for you. It means be normal, be natural, and just do things bigger. Physiology is big. Increasing the size of your gestures in a presentation increases the impact. Think of turning up the volume of your radio. If you were alone listening to the radio, you'd have the volume turned to a normal level; however, if you want the sound to fill the room, you'd turn up the volume. The same goes with your gestures. I have no hard-and-fast rules about body language because it's a completely subjective experience.

Q. Are you saying exterminate the archetypes of presenting?

A. I repeat, exterminate the archetypes of mediocrity. Period. Let yourself shine.

Q. **Do I need to think ahead about moving?**

A. If you're going to move, move with purpose. Think ahead. Don't wander. Walk to a place, and then stop. Do your business, and then move again. If I had a wish for presenters, it would be this: I'd have all presenters learn to love not moving, just being still. It adds much more presence to your presentation. Notice I said still—not rigid. Again, go to www.ted.com and look at the different presenters and their riveting talks. The presentations are by people from all walks of life—scientists, teachers, inventors. Returning to standing still, watch Sir Ken Robinson's talk on how schools kill creativity.

CHAPTER 6

OPEN WITH A BOOM!

Spend the next five minutes scripting out the opening of a presentation. Pick a topic you know well or a recent presentation. In case you're wondering, the opening is what you do or say before you get into the content of your message.

Along with everyone else, I immediately started to craft my opening. It appeared to me that this wasn't one of Brad's key points. I realized he was likely going to ask each of us to make our opening pitch, and he would then critique them. It seemed to me to be the usual stuff: welcome the audience, introduce myself, and let them know my subject. We all finished promptly. After all, it was just an opening to a presentation.

WHAT AUDIENCES WANT

Let's think about what the purpose of your opening is in the bigger scheme of things. Consider your presentation opening from an audience's perspective. Imagine you are sitting at a presentation that has yet to begin. What do you expect and want from the presenter? Here's a list I've put together from my own experiences. This is what people have told me.

- I want to know what it's about.
- I want to like the presenter.

- I want to be engaged.
- I hope to be inspired.
- I want to know what's in it for me.
- I want to feel as if I am going to enjoy it.
- I don't want to feel exposed or singled out.
- I want to feel that it's going to be a good session.
- I want to be entertained.

Here is what listeners don't want:

- I don't want to be bored.
- I don't want it to sound like every other presentation I've heard.
- I don't want to start sleeping the moment the presenter says "good morning."
- I don't want the opening to feel as though it's only being done because it's part of the presentation process and is a necessary evil.
- I don't what the presenter to look bored, frightened, or nervous.
- I don't want to know where the fire exits are.

These are all great and fair things that audiences typically want and don't want from a presenter's opening. With these in mind, now reexamine your opening and ask this question, "Does my opening help me achieve the things I listed in the 'what audiences want' section?"

The silence in the room was deafening. A wave of realization washed over us all. My presentation probably does the opposite. I was feeling picked on even though Brad didn't speak to me directly. It was true my opening did not *do the things he spoke about, but I bet no one's did. After all, there are not many ways to open a presentation. Or are there?*

Who wants to share their opening?

There was an awkward silence, and Brad exploited it. Next, he said what I was thinking.

I'm guessing some of you are feeling uncomfortable about doing this because what you've written doesn't achieve the positive points we've just listed. Don't be troubled. Here's my guess at what most of you have written.

1. Good morning.
2. My name is—
3. I'm from—
4. I'm going to speak to you about—
5. My presentation is going to last—
6. There is no scheduled fire alarm testing today but—

How many people in the room have those six things in an order similar to what I've written?

Almost everyone raised a hand. A couple of people didn't. One guy said that he left out the "good morning" part.

Don't get me wrong. There is nothing wrong with any of that. Would you consider your opening a Thrive, Survive, or Nose-Dive way to open? I suggest it was a Survive way, and what makes it a Survive opening is that it doesn't light up the room. It's pretty normal, and most people start a presentation that way. *Boring. Dull. Blah.*

AVOID DULLNESS

Let's consider the cliché "you never get a second chance to make a first impression" and think about it in relation to the goals of establishing our first impression. Can you see how your goals and what you've written for an opening don't match?

Imagine you are a procurement manager, and today you are sitting in on five presentations of companies that have been short-listed to win a contract with your business. We've already predicted how the five competing presenters will open their presentations. It may sound something like this,

91

Brad drew himself up in a stiff, unnatural manner—a bit like the News Reader archetype.

Good morning, my name is Justin Otherfellow. I'm the managing director of Dullness Incorporated. Thank you for giving us the opportunity to present to you today. I am going to talk about how Dullness Inc. can help you increase your win/lose ratios ahead of the industry average.

That's what everybody says, right? Eighty percent of presenters begin their presentations this way. The result? Mediocrity, sameness, cliché, and little differentiation. *Boring.* No boom in that opening.

We began to understand what Brad was talking about. But how was I personally going to break away from such monotony?

You have to strip away convention and do something different to capture the hearts and minds of your audience. You have to make it easy for them to connect your presentation, not to mention enjoy it.

I'm going to share a formula guaranteed to help you shine in your audience's eyes. I call it the boom opening. By using appropriate words and media, you can be confident attendees will hang on your every word. You'll open your presentation better than 80 percent of your competitors and colleagues. And that will create a meaningful difference for you. Furthermore, the better you get with boom openings, the more you will shine. Let's break down the boom opening into its parts.

THE BOOM OPENING

The first thing you absolutely must do is *get the audience interested in you.* And the quickest and best way to do this, by far, is to use a boom opening. It has seven elements and is usually done sequentially in steps:

1. Make the boom statement.
2. Greet the audience.
3. Introduce yourself.

4. Announce your goal.
5. Engage the audience.
6. Explain the benefits of your message.
7. Go over housekeeping (timing, agenda, protocol).

Below is a graphic that you may find useful.

Opening Checklist

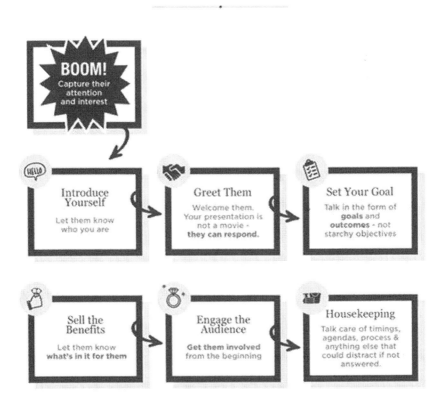

Here are the steps in more detail.

STEP 1. THE BOOM STATEMENT

So the boom statement is something that gets people going; it makes the audience metaphorically respond like alert and interested meerkats.

We laughed as he stood up suddenly, eyes wide, intent, his hands tucked up under his belly, stretching his neck, peering around, just like a meerkat. He presented a picture of a meerkat on the screen.

A boom opening can take many forms. You can compliment the audience; ask a direct question; make a startling statement or use an arresting statistic; use a visual aid; tell a story about a personal experience; cite a higher authority; challenge your audience so they are in conflict; or you can contrast one thing with another. These and other approaches are material for a boom opening. Let's examine the one's I mentioned more closely so that you have a better idea about what I mean.

COMPLIMENT THE AUDIENCE

A genuine thank-you or compliment is a delightful way to break some ice and put the audience and yourself at ease. It actually does more than that: it can create an instant rapport with your audience.

"Ladies and gentlemen, I am thrilled to be given the opportunity to share some ideas with the team that is leading the industry in the Advantage Surveys. You're the team the industry is following."

ASK RHETORICAL QUESTIONS

A rhetorical question is an instant way to create interest and relevance right at the start. It immediately gets people thinking and making a link between what you're presenting and what they want to achieve.

"Would it be useful if I share three proven ideas that will keep the competition away from your customers? Would that be a useful thing to do for the next forty minutes?"

MAKE A STARTLING STATEMENT

People like drama. They like being captured by something big. By making a startling statement, you metaphorically throw cold water over your audience and grab their attention. You wake them up.

"The next presentation you make outside this room could be the difference between you winning or losing your next deal, your next job, or your next promotion."

USE AN INSIGHTFUL STATISTIC

In the advertising world, statistics get used all over the place. Such as this straightforward, simple one: "Half of my advertising is wasted. The problem is, I don't know which half."

Even though we may not believe much what advertisers say, their techniques can be used effectively in opening presentations.

"The last Gallup survey showed that 86 percent of all retailers are looking for innovative ways that enhance their shoppers' experiences at the point of purchase and engage them. Eighty-six percent!"

USE A VISUAL AID

We all know the cliché "A picture is worth a thousand words." A high-quality picture that's associated with what you're talking about can create interest and intrigue. Make sure you only use high-quality graphics. Never ever use clip art.

And try to avoid the temptation of getting images from Google Images for the simple reason that you maybe infringing on copyrights, even though the chances are they won't be unique and the quality will vary. A great place to get original images is www.istockphoto.com, but my personal favorite site is www.fotolia.com. It's not expensive: by spending less than a dollar, you can open your presentation with an original boom. Otherwise, people use www.flickr.com or google images because it's free. The images are generally good but not terribly unique or of professional quality. Also, be careful with the 'free' sites. You may be infringing someone else's copyright and photograph ownership.

SHARE A PERSONAL EXPERIENCE

We all love stories. Sharing a personal story opens a window to your personality that can enable people to connect with you and your topic. It can also demonstrate in an interesting way that you have some experience and expertise in your subject matter.

"Failure is the result of simple little errors done every day. I want to share with you the 'simple little errors' I did every day that cost me my most valuable account to enable all of us here to avoid any future failures with other clients."

REFERENCE A HIGHER AUTHORITY

Professor Robert Cialdini, PhD, highlighted and described one of the most powerful principles of social influence: authority.[2] Quoting authoritative figures has a tribal effect on people. It gives extra credibility and gravitas to whatever you're speaking about. Several examples follow.

"Bill Meaney, our global CEO, recently said that our success and future lies in the hands of our leadership and how we lead going into our new financial year."

"Your new leader, Lou Gerstner, wants to change IBM's sales culture from one that sells mainframes to one that sells technology consulting."

"Our owner and principal wants our private school to transform the way it tests and educates children with learning difficulties such as dyslexia, ADHD, and related issues."

CHALLENGE THE AUDIENCE

There's nothing like throwing out a challenge to an audience to incite some thinking and engagement. This kind of opening works because a lot of

---

5 Cialdini, Robert B., PhD. *Influence: The Psychology of Persuasion.* New York: HarperCollins, 2007.

people in the audience are in an open frame of mind, trying to consciously or unconsciously decide on the value of what you are going to talk about.

"I'm willing to bet that by the end of this presentation you will find three new ways to create, enhance, and maintain great customer engagement."

Story, Metaphor, Humor, and Colin Hall

Make your opening come alive by telling a story. Audiences tend to remember stories with ease.

Colin Hall, the former CEO of a sixty-thousand-person organization called Wooltru in South Africa, is a master storyteller. He fills the room with stories of amazing insight that always have a deeper, relevant meaning to those listening. It's like there are two things going on: at a surface level, there is a very engaging story, and at a deeper level, Colin touches your heart and creates an internal motivation that says, *this really matters.*

Colin opened a leadership meeting with the following introduction and story:

When we think of personal energy, we can think of people who subtract—who take energy away from us. Other people add, and our energy lifts. The very worst are those who divide. They seem to be deliberately destructive. They make trouble; they set one against another; they stretch relationships to breaking point. And then there are the multipliers: those wonderful people who come into our lives and spiral up the energy—infinitely. Somehow they seem to know how to generate huge amounts of positive human energy, which they share abundantly.

The difference between living fully and existing is personal energy. How we feel when we get up in the morning and face the day. How we feel about ourselves, those around us, and the canvas upon which we paint the story of our lives.

There is an apocryphal story about personal energy that is worth telling:

A Spanish gentleman knocks on his son's door. "Jaime," he says, "wake up!" Jaime answers, "I don't want to get up, Papa." The father shouts, "Get up, you have to go to school." Jaime says, "I don't want to go to school." "Why not?" asks the father. "Three reasons," says Jaime. "First, because it's so dull; second, the kids tease me; and third,

I hate school." And the father says, "Well, I am going to give you three reasons why you must go to school. First, because it is your duty; second, because you are forty-five years old; and third, because you are the headmaster!"

Ladies and gentleman, good morning and welcome!

A FEW CAUTIONARY WORDS

Now, a word of caution before we move on. If you're not a storyteller or a joke teller, either learn how to tell stories and jokes, or don't do it. It's one or the other. My advice is learn to tell stories and jokes.

Here's another caution: when you open with your boom statement, *say nothing about you or your content.* Open only with your boom statement. Then, *after* your boom statement, greet the audience—the whole audience—and introduce yourself.

If the very thought of this feels strange, don't worry because you'll be in great company. For instance, how do the news programs start on television? Don't a lot of them start with the key stories of the day to catch your attention so it makes you want to keep listening to them and not channel hop? Don't comedians do the same? They just launch into their routine?

Do you remember the movie *Dead Poets Society* with Robin Williams? Do you remember the carpe diem scene? Everyone who saw that movie does. If you correctly remember that scene, it was about Robin Williams meeting his students for the first time. Extraordinary impact. It is a tremendous example of a boom opening.

AUDIOVISUAL BOOMS

In many conference settings, presenters open with a "video sting." This is a film clip that they have paid to have had made for them—usually it's some customers saying how great they or their brands are, a new product launch or some achievements.

With the Internet and YouTube in particular, there are a lot of no- or low-cost options you can add to your presentations. There is a wide range of clips you can use to create a boom. Simply go onto YouTube and search for a genre.

STEP 2. GREET THE AUDIENCE

After your boom opening, welcome the audience and greet them. Nothing too fancy, just polite and professional or whatever is appropriate to the group you are with. When I do this, I have a few little rules to help me connect more with the audience. When I say good morning or welcome, I make sure I say it slowly rather than just blurting it out. Always have good eye contact with the audience and *smile*. Also leave a space for the audience to respond either vocally or in their heads. You'll be amazed at how many people say good morning back to you. "Ladies and gentlemen, good morning. I'm thrilled to be here this morning."

STEP 3. INTRODUCE YOURSELF

This is the easiest part. Still, people forget to introduce themselves because they get so caught up in their own nervousness. The same tips apply here as they do for greeting people. Politely and clearly let people know who you are, where you're from, and what role you have. Here's my own introduction: "My name is Brad Waldron. I work with a wonderful company called Intelligent Inspiration."

I don't mind if people would prefer to introduce themselves before they greet the audience. It really doesn't matter. It's whatever feels best once you've done it a few times. But please, open with the boom first. You'll be amazed by the impact it has with your audience.

STEP 4. ANNOUNCE YOUR GOAL

Immediately after greeting the audience and introducing yourself, you should tell everyone why you're there. I use the term *goal* rather than *objective* or my *agenda*. I often find stating a goal is much stronger emotionally than stating an objective. There is a place for your agenda but not at this point.

Agendas are not outcome based, whereas introducing a goal helps establish a vision for your presentation and coming material, such as:

"My goal today is to allow us as the senior leadership team to align to one vision and one team that will enable us to create an organization that people will want to belong to."

STEP 5. ENGAGE THE AUDIENCE

After announcing your goal, there can often be a temptation to jump straight into your presentation's content. If you sometimes feel that's the case, press the pause button. There are still opportunities to create deeper rapport with the audience and give you time to think.

Tony Robbins, the famous peak performance coach, says you must lead an audience and take control right from the beginning. The easiest and most respectful way I have found to do this is by engaging the audience. There are several ways to do this. Here are a few effective ways:

- Ask a relevant question.
- Undertake a group activity.

Have your audience call out or write down their goals for attending your presentation.

I find that when I engage with the audience from the beginning of my presentation, it creates greater responsiveness and lasts throughout my presentation. So, engage your audience early.

Here are a few examples I use from time to time, depending on the group, its size, or the seniority of the audience:

I ask a question that has a yes-or-no answer. I may ask, "How many people believe that with better category insights we can produce better solutions for our customers?"

I ask a question that they have to rate on a scale of 1 to 10. They respond by showing me their answers by holding up their fingers to represent their individual answer. It goes like this, "Before I begin, let me ask you a question. On a scale of 1 to 10, where 10 represents highest value for money, what are your customers saying about our new customer-incentive plans in the marketplace?"

I ask people to turn to the person next to them and answer a question. It looks something like this, "Before I begin, please turn to your colleague beside you and answer this question. What is the problem and solution that would allow you to achieve greater speed to market with new product developments?"

I put a slide up with some facts or statistics and get them to comment about them at their tables. This is also a good icebreaker. I might say, "Look at this slide and notice where we sit in the marketplace based on our customers' ratings. At your table please discuss for two minutes what is the one thing, if we could do superbly well, that would allow us to move up the performance scale."

Let's move on to benefits.

STEP 6. EXPLAIN THE BENEFITS OF YOUR MESSAGE

However I may set up my audience in my engagement piece, I link my key points to the benefits in my presentation. This usually keeps my audience interested and lets them know why they should listen. Of course we need to get to those *why* learners right away (remember 4MAT and the four kinds of learning). Here's a typical message benefits explanation.

Some of the benefits you'll get from today's presentation will be as follows:

• You'll know exactly what your customers think of you.
• You'll learn what you can personally do to influence your customers to like you even more.
• You'll learn how to use new market insights to help position your customers' category growth.
• You'll know exactly how I can help XYZ company drive greater market performance.

STEP 7. HOUSEKEEPING

This is the time to share the logistical part of your presentation. For instance, how long your presentation will last, the agenda, where the bathrooms are, time for breaks, how and when to ask questions, what to do in case of a fire alarm, and all the other back-of-the-mind questions people may have. I know a couple of presenters who actually start their presentations with this stuff. While it's important, I have seen the audience start doodling in their pads, checking their phones, going online—disengaging.

OPENINGS TO AVOID

I have a few more tips. Here are openings you should never use, under any circumstances. Don't fall into the hole!

DON'T STATE THE OBVIOUS.

Don't restate the title of the speech or reiterate information. *You need every moment to create interest and suspense.* Don't go over what is already known. Don't start by saying "I'm going to talk to you today about safety."

DON'T OPEN YOUR PRESENTATION WITH AN APOLOGY.

Pay attention. You may think it makes you sound friendly and not arrogant, but apologies set up your audience to listen for your weaknesses.

DON'T READ YOUR OPENING (WHETHER IT'S ON THE SCREEN OR IN YOUR NOTES).

You'll miss connecting with your audience from the beginning, plus they will also think that you are either very nervous or underprepared. Leave the clichés for the competition. For instance, here's a no-no: "Good morning, my name is Justin Otherfellow. I'm the managing director of Dullness Incorporated. Today I am going talk to you about shades of gray. The presentation will conclude at eleven, at which point there will be time for questions and answers over coffee."

After that start, the loud sound you will hear from your audience is snoring!

MOVING ON

By the way, this is only my opening. It takes anywhere from thirty seconds to three minutes. I've still got my whole presentation in front of me.

So, you hit it off with a boom statement, greet the audience, introduce yourself, explain your goal, engage the audience, point out the benefits you have to offer, and now you're ready to begin your presentation.

When done properly, opening your next presentation using this exciting seven-step approach will provide the following benefits:

- The audience will feel excited and interested.
- It will help you set the pace.
- You will gain confidence right from the beginning.
- The audience will know what's in it for them.
- It will distinguish you from your competitors.

JACQUI

The National Sales Awards sponsored by the Sales and Marketing Management Association in the UK is a prestigious affair. Salespeople across all industries have an opportunity to demonstrate their professionalism by entering this annual competition. The process is straightforward but thorough. You simply fill out an eighteen-page document that actually translates into a customer case study, and depending on the criteria the judges are looking for, you either get a letter thanking you for entering, or you get invited to present before a varied panel of sales experts. Recently, Jacqui from a pharmaceutical company made the short list. Jacqui and seven others from handpicked industries had the opportunity to impress the judges and demonstrate their sales expertise.

A colleague of mine was one of the judges. So I asked her how the judges decided. She said, "The fact is everyone who is presenting has already won because they have demonstrated exceptional account management skills. On the day of the presentations, we see every candidate—one after the other. So hopefully the winner will stand out for us."

Jacqui worked for Kate (you met her in chapter one), and Kate asked me to help Jacqui prepare and rehearse for her big day. When we got together, Jacqui had the bare bones of a presentation that was effectively a client case study. After watching Jacqui diligently run through it, I realized there was enough content to blow away the judges. However, her style was very meek, and her content was not sequenced in a way that took people on a journey.

The two things we did together was reorganize and reenergize her content. We gave it some life and structured it using the 4MAT. With that firmly in place, we wrapped a theme around the presentation: the theme was a "Leadership Approach to Selling," and we decided to use an apple as visual theme to open the presentation with.

When Jacqui opened her presentation with a boom, this is what she said, "When I thinking of selling from a salesperson's perspective, I compare it to this apple. The apple is my client, and my goal is to get inside the apple and get as many seeds as I can. The seeds available represent client revenue. That's great thinking if I was just a salesperson. However, if I put the hat on of a sales leader, I'd ask a better question. I would take out a seed and ask my clients, 'How many apples can we grow together from this seed?'" Immediate game changer. Jacqui went into her presentation using the 4MAT as the template structure.

Three months later the association held its awards night at the Grosvenor House Hotel in London's world famous Park Lane. Jacqui was there, and she didn't know how she had done. The night drew on slowly as she waited patiently for the winner to be announced. The time had come to announce her category. The presenter of the awards was Paul Ross, a British television and radio presenter, journalist, and nationally known media personality. He announced the finalists. He said, "The winner of this category broke all traditions in presenting her case by capturing the judge's imagination with a dissected apple. Ladies and gentlemen, the winner of National Account Manager of year is Jacqui."

We were ecstatic! Thirty-five categories won that night. Only in Jacqui's category did the host presenter talk about the quality of the presentation. We had three people in the finals, and we walked away with three titles. The first time ever for my client.

It just goes to show that when it comes down to it, some presenters can establish an unfair advantage when the competition is tight.

FREQUENTLY ASKED QUESTIONS

Q. Opening—the first few minutes of a presentation, a training, or an interview—fill me with dread. Don't you find it the same way?

A. No, because I've learned what's at stake and how to handle myself. You can do the same thing. I agree that there is a lot at stake, and the following adage is an important one: *You never get a second chance to make a first impression.*

Let's break it down. Here are five things your audience wants right off the bat: (1) They want to know what your presentation is about. (2) They hope to like you. (3) They want to be engaged—there's little worse than being bored. (4) They even want to be inspired. (5) And they definitely want to know what the takeaways are for them personally. Make sure your opening achieves and promises those.

Q. Can I avoid dullness?

A. Strip away convention and do something different to capture the hearts and minds of your audience. You have to make it easy for them to experience your presentation, not to mention enjoy it. The first thing you absolutely must do is *get the audience interested in you.* Learn how to do a boom opening, particularly a boom statement. It will get everyone—you and your audience—on the same map.

Q. What is the main thing about a boom statement?

A. The boom statement is something that gets people going; it makes the audience sit up and know something different—something not dull—is about to take place and perhaps they might want to pay attention, and it can take several forms.

Q. What's the advantage of a startling statement?

A. *People like drama.* They like being drawn into something big, especially if it's based on facts. Making a startling statement is energizing, and it grabs your attention. Your audience focuses and pays attention. For example, "The next presentation you make outside this room could be the difference between you winning or losing your next deal, your next job, or your next promotion." Sales and marketing people are likely to respond—positively.

CHAPTER 7

END WITH A BANG

This is the way the world ends,
Not with a bang but with a whimper.

—T. S. ELIOT

Imagine reading a book with the last chapter missing, seeing a musical without a memorable closing number, or watching an action film that ends passively. You'd feel shortchanged! Your presentations, talks, and interviews should not end with a whimper. Ideally, they end with a *bang*, rousing your audience to action and commitments.

In the world of presenting, a lot of presentation endings simply aren't compelling, and that's usually because the presenter's focus was on content instead of on a call for action and the "here's the one thing I want people to remember" element. Closing about what you want people to think, do, and believe as a consequence of your presentation. That really matters. You must end your presentation with a bang, not a whimper. That's what this chapter is about.

THE IMPORTANCE OF CLOSING WELL

People tend to remember more about the last thing they heard than about the middle of a talk. Yet the majority of speakers just fade away when they get to the end of their talks. I've seen people so relieved their stint on the podium is almost over that they start to pack up before they finish speaking. So, too, are their audiences.

A chuckle ran through the class. I, for one, was laughing at Brad's section on closings because in past presentations I would rank myself as inept, mostly because I hadn't thought about closing with a bang. I wasn't trained.

Powerful speakers save a lot of energy and concern for the audience until the end, and they make their conclusions taste like a scrumptious dessert, something delicious that leaves a memorable aftertaste.

I realize this may sound frivolous, but I don't mean to be. I can't emphasize enough the need to close your presentation as strongly as possible. Imagine that you've created a wonderful opening and put together an artful body of content, but your closing line consists of two words, "Any questions?" That's like telling a joke without a punch line or, worse still, the wrong punch line!

For example, "Ladies and gentlemen, thank you for your time this morning. In going forward, if there are any questions about my proposal, please do not hesitate to contact me." How was that? It's professional, but it's still not effective. Aren't you trying to differentiate yourself and not sink further into the blur of forgetful presentations?

CEMENT A CONNECTION

You need a bang close. You need another naked moment. What can you give the audience as a bang takeaway? Closing is just as easy as an opening, but in a close you can be more adventurous. An opening is quite structured because you've literally got seconds to help people form an appropriate opinion of you and your presentation. The close is different. You can have more of a poetic license to be more varied in your close. Exceptional presenters will finish in a way that links all of their key points together and cements a connection with their audience's hearts and minds. It takes time, thinking, and practice. This is the stuff that will really differentiate you.

A HIGHWAY MOMENT

Andrew Cowan is a leader of people, a real leader, not just someone who's only responsible for delivering the profit and loss of a company. He knows that the profit and loss of a business ultimately resides in the hearts and minds of those he leads. He describes closing a presentation as a highway moment.

Imagine this, you're the country managing director of the world's largest alcoholic drinks company. You see dozens of presentations from different staff, suppliers, and clients. On Friday afternoon, you are driving home on the highway, and you're reflecting on your week. In the quietness of your own mind, you think of that man or that woman who made an impact with you with their presentation. They had the right messages and the right product and product strategies, but most of all, they had that spark in their presentation. And the way they closed their presentation made for a compelling reason to place the business with them. That's a highway moment. That's the impact of a Naked Presentation with a shining close.

Ask, "What do I want my audience thinking and feeling when I close my presentation?" Whatever the answer is, that's how you must write and design a close with a bang. It's the most respectable thing to do for your audience rather than leave it to a random opportunity or even worse—a cliché close.

ICING ON THE CAKE

Your conclusion must tie in with your opening and your overall purpose. Your ending must connect naturally with your beginning, and that's where presentation structure continues to be important. Conclusions are the way you make your presentation look, sound, and feel complete.

NEVER ANNOUNCE YOUR INTENTION TO CONCLUDE

A word of warning. If people get much advance notice that you are going to conclude, in their mind they'll wind up your speech and start to tune you out. Your audience will disengage, start packing up, cell phones will be turned on. You've lost. So much for your concluding points.

Be more subtle. Lead into your conclusion with a creative transition instead of the not very dynamic "And so in conclusion, I would like to reiterate the importance of sitting properly on chairs because back safety is important. Thank you very much. Are there any questions?"

THE BANG CLOSE

We generally know the things that haven't worked, the things that made people leave mentally before you were finished. So, let's look at what *does* work.

If this was a big Broadway musical, this is your critical point, your final number, the big finale. The bang close. However, in a presentation, it's where you ask for what you want. People will listen to you. Below is a graphic describing a six-step simple process—things your close must do in order to be effective. If your close has all of these things, you're the gold standard.

CLOSING CHECKLIST

Take time and make sure you include the following approach. It will serve you well and help you do a bang close.

Closing Checklist

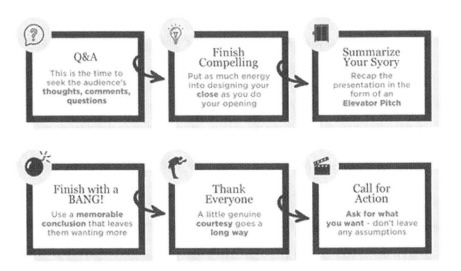

FIVE BANG ENDINGS THAT WORK

There are no hard-and-fast rules about what type of bang to use. I'm sure the list of effective bangs is endless. Personally, I find the following five types provide a useful set of closing ingredients.

1. DEMONSTRATE THE VALUE OF THE PRESENTATION

Summarize key points of your presentation to clarify its value to the audience. You can frame the information either positively or negatively.

A POSITIVE (PLEASURE) FRAME

- The vision of the opportunity

- The value of the vision
- The positive consequences of achieving the vision
- The solution

A NEGATIVE (PAIN) FRAME

- Define the problem you're solving.
- Quantify and qualify the size of the problem: if you place a cost that is linked to the problem it often generates much more commitment.
- The consequences of not solving the problem in the short and long term
- The solution

2. LINK BACK TO YOUR OPENING

People do like consistency. By referring back to the beginning of your presentation, you create a natural feeling of closure and it "proves" you have hit your presentation objectives.

3. USE A FILM CLIP, POEM, OR QUOTE

Using a motivational film, poem, or quote will create an emotional connection between your presentation and the message of the clip.

At a recent Diageo conference in Ireland, the on-trade director Keiran Budds showed a powerful speech delivered by Al Pacino from the movie *Any Given Sunday*. He had everyone stand and huddle up while the clip was being screened. It was enormously powerful. If you haven't seen it yet, go and search on YouTube for "Pacino speech Any Given Sunday."

4. USE A STORY OR METAPHOR

Use a story to demonstrate the key relevance of your presentation or to demonstrate the value of what you're saying. Here's an example a sales director used at a quarterly sales conference to motivate the sales team:

"Every morning on the African savannah, a lion wakes up. It knows it must outrun and outthink an impala just to stay alive. On that same morning an impala also wakes up and it knows it must outrun and outthink a lion just to stay alive. It really doesn't matter if you see yourself as a powerful lion or a graceful impala, make sure when you wake up tomorrow after this conference you are outrunning and outthinking the competition."

5. ISSUE A CHALLENGE

Issuing the audience a challenge is often a great way to incite action from a presentation.

Here is an example of a challenge used at a monthly sales team meeting:

"Based on last month's performance numbers it is easy to see where we are delivering solid overall performance and ignore what's not working well. But we can't have that. This month, starting tomorrow, I need everyone in this room to be personally responsible for smashing their target in our weakest performing product line. My challenge to everyone is simple. I need every member of this team to sell five websites on top of our other performance targets."

HAVE ENOUGH ENERGY TO FINISH STRONGLY

When I was a small boy, my father taught me how to run. I used to love going to athletic meets. Every year in high school I would win the 100, 200, 400, hurdles, long jump, triple jump, shot put, and the relay. I'd even get a place in the discus and javelin. I was an athlete who thrived on the explosive events where pure energy, strength, and technique pulled me over the finish line, usually in first place.

The 800 and 1,500 meter races perplexed me. Though the distance included a sprint, it also required a strategy, and I can still hear my father's advice echoing loudly in my mind, "Make sure you have enough juice in your tank to finish strong—stronger than your start." You'll notice I said I got a place in those strategy events and not a gold. That's because I didn't listen to my dad's advice. I didn't finish those distance races strongly; I finished with whatever energy I had left. It was never enough.

That's my encouragement to you. Always have enough energy to finish strongly. Otherwise, you may miss your gold medal. Close your great presentations with an ending that's distinctly you, something that will capture your audience's attention and hearts and compel them to take action—whether it be to hire you, buy your services or products or support you in a project.

I sometimes close my presentations with a story about Pig and Molly. This true story is my "close with a bang" ending chapter for this book.

FREQUENTLY ASKED QUESTIONS

Q. **I get the end-with-a-bang bit, but why did you say never announce your intention to conclude?**

A. If people get an advance warning that you're going to conclude, they mentally wind up your speech and start tuning you out. Just watch the energy in a room the next time you hear someone announce their intention to conclude. At the very least, you will see and hear a lot of shuffling—people closing notepads and unzipping bags. Some will start e-mailing; others will text or use Twitter. Some will find excuses for leaving and be disruptive.

Keep your audience alert and deliver a good conclusion. And remember that a good conclusion needs a lot of energy. It may be a stirring statement, a joke, or a call to action. Some conclusions try to motivate by directly challenging the audience.

Q. **I facilitate a lot of corporate trainings, and I find it's difficult to get attendees to stop texting and e-mailing. What can I do?**

A. One colleague of mine simply stops talking. Eventually, the other attendees put enough pressure on them so they stop. I sometimes let individual instances go, but during my opening, I always set up ground rules, which then allows me to ask people to stop texting. I say something like, "I recognize everyone in this room has pressing agendas, and your colleagues, customers, and suppliers all want a piece of you while you're here with me today. I'd be grateful if we could all make a commitment. I'll commit to giving you a lot of breaks to check voice messages and e-mails, if you resist the temptation to check your messages while we are working together." If everyone has agreed to this, it gives me permission to hold people accountable if they start checking their voice messages while in session with me.

Q. **What ingredients make a bang close?**

A. Put as much energy into your close as you did your opening. Summarize your key messages. Take any comments or questions (if appropriate). Include a bang statement. Thank the attendees and organizers. And, importantly, make a call for action. Action is the stuff of drama.

CHAPTER 8

PIG AND MOLLY

I wish I was half the person my dogs think I am.

Whenever I go away from home for a period of time, people hear me talk about my two dogs. I inherited them, Pig and Molly. They're English bull terriers. They're not the type of dogs that are considered to be attractive.. Nobody says, "Oh, aren't they cute." Quite the contrary. When I take them for walks, people cross to the other side of the road to avoid them.

I laughed. The whole class laughed, taken aback by this sudden change in Brad's attitude, though his tone remained affectionate.

On several occasions, I've tried to give Molly away, but no one will have her. However, secretly, if anyone did say, "Yeah, I'll have her," I'd say, well, I was only kidding!

They're not known for their ability to be gentle. They stink! Recently, while I was taking Molly for a walk, I heard a small child ask her mommy, "Mom why is that man walking a goat?"

Again, we laughed.

Molly has the most annoying habit of wiping her nose on any part of exposed skin you have. You may be sitting outside in the sun on a reclining lounge with your shirt off, and Molly will stealthy come up beside you and drag her wet nose along your ribs.

There was more laughter and a few disgusted groans.

That's just Molly. Pig has his own deplorable habits that defy mentioning.

Brad grinned. We were all laughing by now, seeing that Brad was building a good story.

But when I'm away I miss them. And I can't wait to get home because I know that I'm going to be greeted in a special way. The moment my key goes in the door, what do you think I'm going to hear?

What? somebody in the audience shouted, caught up in Brad's story.

Grrr. Their growl has the depth of a Harley-Davidson motorcycle. In fact, it sounds like there are two Harleys on the other side of my front door!

Again, total laughter.

That's what I hear. And I say, Pig, it's me! Still I hear *grrr!*

Brad rolled his eyes. Before he could continue, he had to wait for us to stop laughing.

But I go inside anyway. And I call "Pig! Pig, here boy!" Then all of a sudden, it's different, and he does cartwheels and spins around and goes crazy. And it doesn't matter what sort of day Pig's had. He could have been just sitting there doing nothing all day. Bored out of his mind. He could have driven my wife to distraction with disobedience and spent most of the day outside. But the mere fact that I've come home gets him excited and he's beside himself. Molly's the same.

It's an unconscious law for them, for all dogs. They don't know how to be anything other than to be excited. *And I wish that I was half the person Pig really thinks I am.* Because I'm not that person. Sometimes I am, but I'm mostly not, because I'm just a guy doing his daily thing. But for some reason I'm really special to these two dogs. They would do anything for me. That's a loyalty you can't buy. You can only get it through your relationship with them.

Could you imagine that in a workplace? Where people treat you the way that your dog does when you turn up for work? That would be pretty weird, wouldn't it? You'd turn up in the morning, they'd be in the office, they'd just be doing their stuff, at their workstation, and then suddenly they spot your car pulling up into the parking lot. They would all run to the window to see that you've arrived and run back and forth. And as you walk down the hallway, they're all jumping around and trying to get your undivided attention.

But the truth of the matter is that the greatest similarity between most employees and a dog is that they sometimes both stick their noses where they shouldn't. Do you know what I mean?!

A roar of laughter followed Brad's witty observation. I have a vivid imagination, and his picture of my office colleagues rushing to the windows and running around in joy because I arrived—utterly comical. But I also thought, Wouldn't that be wonderful? Game changing. World changing.

A PRESENTER'S GOAL

Presenters are the same. Your goal—one of them, a secret wishing one—is to have your audience thinking of you the same way your dog greets you.

Whether you're going to a meeting or a quarterly conference, you want your audience excited when they find out that you will be presenting. You want them to remember your last presentation; you want them eager to see you again. You want to hear, "That's so cool! At least we know it's not going to be boring."

That's what a skilled presenter invokes in an audience. A skilled presenter accomplishes this through acquired skilled—a very few do it because they intuitively know what to do. A Naked Presenter can create that effect just by being in the room. And that is my invitation to you: find ways to draw out these feelings from your audience because that's what it means to be a presenter who can stand *naked*.

Light up the room—it's what you were born to do.

ABOUT BRAD WALDRON

Brad leads Intelligent Inspiration – a global training and development company that delivers exceptional thought leadership and strategic development solutions.

With a prestigious client list including Sony, Microsoft, Fujitsu, McCann Worldgroup, Diageo, Iron Mountain, BlackRock, Barclaycard, L'Oreal, Redken NYC, Warner Bros, and Yell.com, Intelligent Inspiration understands and delivers leading solutions specializing in:

- Personal Effectiveness
- Sales Performance
- Teams and Leadership
- Culture and Change
- Conferences and Events

For further information on Present Naked or any of our other services offerings contact Brad and Intelligent Inspiration.

Web: www.IntelligentInspiration.com
Email: Brad@IntelligentInspiration.com
Twitter: @bradwaldron

GET YOUR RESOURCES, TOOLS AND TEMPLATES

For all the activities and templates that can help you put together and deliver a naked presentation can be found at this website. Enjoy!

www.PresentNaked.com

Made in the USA
Charleston, SC
29 June 2015